GUIDE
TO EFFECTIVE
STUDY

2

GUIDE
TO EFFECTIVE
STUDY

Richard A. Kalish

California School for Professional Psychology

Brooks/Cole Publishing Company
Monterey, California
A Division of Wadsworth, Inc.

Printed in the United States of America

10 9 8

Library of Congress Cataloging in Publication Data

Kalish, Richard A
    Guide to effective study.

    First-2d ed. published under title: Making the most of
college.
    Bibliography: p. 180
    Includes index.
    1. Study, Method of. I. Title.
LB2395.K3   1979   378.1'7'028   78-32025
ISBN 0-8185-0338-6

Acquisition Editor: Claire Verduin
Project Development Editor: Ray Kingman
Production Editor: Cece Munson
Interior and Cover Design: Ruth Scott
Typist: Elizabeth J. Ritter

PREFACE

Books proposing to help students improve their study skills and enhance their college performance range from the preachy to the practical, from the adjustment-focused to the skills-focused, from the general to the specific. This book addresses these goals from the practical, the skills-focused, and the specific approaches.

The essential principles of effective study haven't changed much since the 1930s, when Francis Robinson was developing the SQ3R method for reading textbooks, an approach that still forms the basis for many study-skills programs. Although the principles remain the same, students have changed. Perhaps more like the students of 20 or 30 years ago, and less like those of the late 1960s and early 1970s, today's students are asking for substance and practicality in their education. They seem to desire to learn, perhaps largely to improve their position in an increasingly competitive job market. Community colleges are playing an increasingly significant role in higher education as more students pursue vocational careers. The backgrounds of the students have changed as well. Today's student enrollments contain more women, more members of ethnic or minority groups, and more older students.

One of my goals in writing *Guide to Effective Study* was to reach this diverse student audience. The chapters on time schedules and principles of learning reflect the fact that many students are single parents or are working full-time. Married, separated, and divorced students are common, and problems of child care or care for elderly parents are as familiar as dating problems once were. Fitting classes in around a part- or a full-time job is very much a a part of scheduling.

My guiding principle in writing this book was to be both *realistic* and *flexible*. I know from experience that, in the short run, the procedure described in this book may take students longer and require more effort than their previous ways of studying. I also know from experience that the effectiveness of a given procedure cannot be adequately evaluated until that procedure has been used for a period of time. Once the students have learned how to apply these procedures, they can modify them, or even replace them altogether, to build their own individual techniques for effective study.

Not only have I attempted to develop a book that is sensitive to differing student preferences for improving study skills, but I have also designed it to appeal to students in a variety of settings. The book can be used by students in a regular credit course, by students working totally independently, or by students enrolled through a counseling center, learning center, extension course, or any of the other more recent programs aimed at enhancing study capabilities.

The sequence in which the chapters in this book can be studied is quite flexible. For students in a formal classroom setting, I would encourage following the chapter sequence as it stands, allowing from one to two weeks per chapter. For students who are working independently, I suggest beginning with a brief reading of the first chapter followed by a more careful reading of the principles of effective study in Chapter 4. It will be worthwhile for each student to consider his or her own individual study problems and to concentrate on the chapters focussing on those specific areas of concern. I believe it's important for the students to consider the exercises as an integral part of their program of effective study.

Students who are working with guidance but are not in a formal classroom program will probably need to orient their progress to that suggested by their instructor. I think that there is a definite advantage to a student working on the same tasks that other students are working on; the interplay will enrich the learning of all concerned.

I want to thank a number of people for their help with this book, as well as those who participated in the two previous editions. They include Laraine Combs, College of the Sequoias; Eleanor Heffernan, Yakima Valley College; Jonathan Lambert, Rockland Community College; Patricia Rizzolo, Pennsylvania State College, Ogontz; and Sue Tweedy, Louisiana State University, all of whom reviewed the manuscript at various stages of development. I also want to acknowledge George Weigand and Arthur Dole, who, when we were all much younger, enabled me to realize that study methods was as legitimate a pursuit for a psychologist as the topics we had been taught in our formal coursework.

Richard A. Kalish

CONTENTS

GUIDE
TO EFFECTIVE
STUDY

OBJECTIVES

1. To provide an introduction to the contents and concepts of this book.

2. To encourage you to be realistic, to set your goals a little too high, to be flexible, and to accept personal responsibility.

3. To discuss the meaning of college and how this meaning has changed over the years.

4. To encourage you to evaluate your definition of "success."

Chapter 1

Introducing This Book

All study problems can be readily solved by a careful reading and an appropriate use of the materials in this book.

What was your reaction to that sentence? "I didn't realize that I could solve my study problems so easily." Or: "That just can't be true, but I should check to see if the book offers anything of value." Or: "What a lot of nonsense—effective study requires long, hard, dull hours and there's no way around it."

In a world filled with claims and counterclaims, propaganda and exaggeration, college students have learned to be on guard against impossible promises. The experts have not found easy ways to get people to lose weight, stop smoking, love their neighbor, or obey the Ten Commandments—nor have they found universally acceptable methods of solving everyone's study problems.

However, certain principles and certain techniques have proved very helpful to students in their academic work. Some of these principles and techniques have been derived from research into the psychology of learning and related matters; some have evolved from long experience in working with students; some are based on the success of only a few individuals.

The ultimate goal of this book is for you to be able to make good use of the text material. I have tried to adhere to certain principles of common sense. You, as a reader, may wish to consider these guiding principles for yourself as well.

First, *be realistic*. There is little point in establishing study programs that you can never fulfill or in making overwhelming demands on yourself—demands that are too great even to contemplate.

Second, *set your goals* a little too high. Expecting much too much can often spell frustration and disappointment, but being satisfied with too little makes you less than you should be. A textbook that never extends its readers' horizons and students who never extend their own horizons are not fulfilling their obligations to themselves.

Third, *be flexible*. A textbook must be written for large numbers of people, but it should be written so that each reader can get from the book whatever he or she finds helpful. Try not to follow rigidly or to reject rigidly the ideas in any book without evaluating them for yourself.

Fourth, *accept responsibility*. You need to recognize that, even though you are to a large extent a product of your earlier home environment, community, and culture, in the last analysis what you do is your own responsibility. You must eventually do something with your life, establish your own goals, and decide on methods of achieving these goals.

This book will not solve all your study problems. However, it can help you learn both general principles and specific techniques that will improve your study effectiveness. And, perhaps, like one student I had many years ago, you may be able to say "I don't know exactly what I learned in your program, and I'm not sure exactly how much of it I use, but taking that course gave me a lot of self-confidence. I use some of your approaches, and I feel that I have something to hang on to—I'm not just grabbing in the dark."

THE MEANING OF COLLEGE

There was a time when people went to college as soon as they finished high school or else they seldom went at all. Colleges were, with very few exceptions, four-year institutions, emphasizing the arts, letters, and sciences, and students were, again with few exceptions, between 17 and 23 years of age. And, except in a few fields such as education and home economics, they were primarily men.

Things changed after World War II, and the changes not only have continued but seem to have accelerated in the last few years. More and more women now attend college. Increasing numbers of students are members of ethnic and racial groups that previously had been rarely represented. And more and more new fields of study have opened up.

The rapid increase in the number and proportion of college students during the 1960s was due, in large part, to the growth of community colleges. Many students are seeking technical and vocational skills rather than the broader education available at four-year colleges. Vocational students, of course, take some liberal-arts courses, but their academic program is directed mainly

at acquiring particular skills for particular jobs. These jobs
range from computer specialist to beautician to psychological
technician to paint chemist to nurse to funeral director. At one
time on-the-job training was sufficient for these fields, but today
more and more persons are pursuing Associate of Arts degrees in
community colleges to improve their competence.

The greatest very recent change has been in the age of entering students. Many older people are now in regular attendance at
community and four-year colleges and universities. By "older," I
mean a range in ages from the late 20s to the late 60s and occasionally beyond. Some of these students are women whose children
are older and who return to school for the education they had
previously interrupted or postponed. Another group of older students consists of people who are working full-time and who wish to
upgrade their job skills or promotion potential through additional
course work. Then, of course, there are the people who want an
outlet from their work—a chance to spend a few hours a week exploring old or new interests. Others attend college as an alternative to work and plan to eventually leave their jobs altogether and
enter what they consider to be a more desirable field of endeavor.

Another group deserves mention—those older students who have
retired from their careers and have more leisure time available.
They may be working toward a degree, but for the most part they are
pursuing particular interests, and neither grades nor credits have
much meaning for them.

Younger students, coming to college straight from high school,
must learn to deal with new freedoms. No one is there to watch over
them; the number of hours of class is reduced; college faculty are
usually more difficult to find outside of class hours than were
high school teachers; the students are now permitted to do poorly
without a note being sent home. Older students may find that college provides less freedom than they are used to. It has been a
long time since they spent many hours a week sitting and listening
to someone else talk; they are accustomed to speaking their minds
and are not intimidated by faculty members.

A 60-year-old person entering a community college as a freshman is motivated by somewhat different factors than is a 19-year-
old. Younger students may be in college because their parents want
them to go or because they don't want to get a job or because of
the social life available. Older students are much more likely to
have a clear picture of why they are in college and what they want
from college.

Sometimes people ask whether older students have more trouble
learning academic material than younger students have. Research
points out that differences are small or nonexistent until the
later years, perhaps the 60s or 70s (see overview in Kalish, 1975).

When learning does seem to become more difficult, it may be because
the older person has more things to distract him or her than a
younger person has. What is more important is that older people,
including those past the age of retirement, can learn just as much
from a college course as younger students, although they sometimes
need to spend a little more time reading and studying. However,
they often compensate for this by their wider experience and
greater maturity, as well as their stronger motivation.

Most study skills are applicable to all students, regardless
of age or sex or ethnicity or anything else (although students with
physical handicaps or those who have limited use of English do face
additional problems). Nonetheless, different conditions require
various modifications. Students who are also working full-time and
students with children to care for confront different problems in
scheduling their time or finding a quiet place to study. Although
the basic principles for effective study are the same, each individual must adapt the materials in this book to meet her or his own
individual needs.

SUCCESS IN COLLEGE

Each individual has a unique definition for success in college.
For some people, grades are the most important basis for judging
success. For others, the completion of college, regardless of
grades, is the major criterion. Still others emphasize learning;
understanding more about the world, themselves, and others; developing job skills or the ability to make lots of money or important
friends; contributing to better family relationships; or becoming
a better citizen.

College success, for most of us, is probably a combination of
all of the above criteria, but the importance of each varies with
the individual. And the importance of each varies across time also,
so that the initial reasons that brought you to college may not be
the most compelling reasons for remaining in college two or three
years later.

The Importance of Grades

The use of grades to measure success in college may well
trouble you. Grades are, of course, only a rough measure of learning. The difficulty is that grades are a part of a system of rewards and punishments that is present throughout the educational
system in this country.

Grades do have several purposes. They give you a chance to evaluate yourself and a chance to see how your instructors are evaluating you. They also permit others, such as prospective employers, to evaluate your potential (this is a major cause of tension concerning grades), and they motivate you to work harder.

Although many faculty members encourage students to place less emphasis on grades, this becomes difficult when both the self-concept and the regard of others depend so much on grades. But it is important to put grades in the proper perspective. First, grades do not signify your worth as a human being, but only your level of performance in one sphere of your life. Second, grades are merely a rough estimate of ability. Third, after you have had work experience, grades become much less important than job performance. Fourth, except for borderline students, one grade in one course rarely has an important influence on anyone's life. And, fifth, people are evaluated all their lives by others—employers, spouses, parents, children, neighbors, and coworkers—and few if any of these evaluations are more objective and fair than the college grades you receive.

For better or for worse, it seems as though grades are here to stay. Hopefully you can avoid worrying about grades per se and concentrate on the task of learning.

Judging Your Own Success

You need to evaluate your success in college for yourself. You also need to evaluate how important to you college success is. You will find that college will compete with pressures from other areas of your life for your time, and your energy, and your money: you want to get to work right away to gain more autonomy; you want to earn money rather than restricting your immediate work possibilities because of your class schedule; you want to spend more time with your family or friends; you want to travel extensively.

College is often seen as part of a program of deferred gratification. That is, college is seen as preparation for the future rather than as something that can be enjoyed in the present. For you to be most successful in college, it will be useful if you can find ways to enjoy both the academic and the nonacademic processes of college for their own sake. College should not be merely a time period to be gotten through but a time period that affords pleasure.

SUMMARY OF IMPORTANT IDEAS

1. It is possible to learn principles and techniques that will
    actually have a meaningful impact on study effectiveness.
2. The four guiding principles for effective study are: be real-
    istic, set goals a little too high, be flexible, and accept
    personal responsibility.
3. The meaning of college has changed over time.
4. Compared to colleges of 75 years ago, today's colleges have
    more women students, more older students, more students from
    ethnic minorities, and more vocational students.
5. Each individual must define college success for himself or
    herself.

EXERCISES

Write an essay that addresses each of the following topics:

1. your reasons for being in college,
2. what you expect to get out of college,
3. your reasons for being in this course, and
4. what you expect to get out of this course.

Your instructor will tell you more about how he or she wants
this essay to be handled—for example, in regard to length and
style. At the end of the course, you may be asked to review this
essay and write another one, discussing any changes in your reasons
for being in college and your feelings about whether your initial
expectations concerning college and this course are being fulfilled.

OBJECTIVES

1. To encourage you to be aware of your college—
    its physical plant, its regulations, and its
    activities.

2. To help you consider major fields of concen-
    tration and to provide some information about
    selecting courses.

3. To get you started thinking about where
    you'll go after you have finished with your
    work at this college.

Chapter 2

Introducing Your Campus

When we talk about "the college campus," we are really talking about a great variety of places where a great variety of objectives are being met. Colleges and universities vary in size from those with a couple of hundred students and a handful of faculty to those with 30,000 or more students and many hundreds of faculty members. They may be in the downtown section of large cities or in isolated rural areas. They may be operated by a branch of government (city, county, or state), or they may be operated under private endowment or by religious groups.

Nor is the task of the institution of higher education limited to teaching students. Research is a responsibility of many faculty members, and some universities have large numbers of full-time professional research people. Colleges also offer services to the local communities through a great variety of extension courses. For example, colleges provide refresher courses for tax accountants and engineers, professional self-improvement programs for nursing-home administrators and teachers, and personal self-improvement courses for anyone in the community who is interested. Larger institutions even have consulting programs for retirement planning, for improving sensitivity to employee needs, and for better police/community relationships. Many programs are offered to agriculture and business by the larger universities.

YOUR CAMPUS

Colleges today offer a fantastic variety of services to their students, ranging from on-campus barbershops (somehow students always complain about the barbers) to a variety of eating places

(students always complain about the food) to a women's center. In
larger colleges, the range of services is so great that many students are unaware of all of the services they are eligible to
receive.

Becoming Familiar with the Physical Plant

After the first few days on even the largest of campuses, you
will have learned how to get to your classrooms, the cafeteria, the
bookstore, some of the dormitories, and certain social areas, such
as the student union. You will also have learned a few short cuts
and, if you drive to school, a bit about where you can find a park-
ing space most readily at the hours you arrive on campus.

However, if your campus is large, much still remains that you
have not yet located. You may still be uncertain about how to get
to the campus medical facilities, the faculty offices, the business
office, the job placement center, the counseling center, the campus
police office, or the office of the Dean of Students. Such knowledge can usually be obtained as you need it, but you will save time
and confusion later by noticing those buildings you do not enter
and finding out what offices they contain.

If you attend a community college, you should find out whether
your school has a general center that brings together the library,
audiovisual resources (including computerized aids for learning),
and other resources. Increasing numbers of colleges are now providing these services under one organization, and it will be extremely useful to know what you can find there and how you can most
effectively use available services and materials.

Campus Regulations

Every campus has academic regulations that play an important
part in day-to-day campus living. Examples of these regulations are
procedures for preregistration, time allowed to make up an "Incomplete," and alternatives you have when you feel a particular regulation has been inappropriately applied. Perhaps the most important
regulations are those governing credits, grading, entering and
dropping courses, and so forth. Whether the accumulation of course
credits is really the best criterion for awarding a degree is debatable—perhaps a series of comprehensive written and oral examinations would be preferable—but colleges in the United States
follow the credits plus grade-point-ratio system, and you should
know your school's variations. When can you drop a class without
risking a failing grade? When does your college place a student on

academic probation, and how long does he or she have to get off?
Does three years of high school math absolve you of having to take
college math? Can you get credits for supervised work experience?
Are there courses you can take on a pass/fail basis rather than a
standard grading basis? What happens to your credits toward graduation if you change your major from elementary education to office
management? If you repeat a course you previously failed and get a
C, how is your grade-point ratio determined?

Campus Activities

What is the value of participating in nonacademic activities
on campus? What are the disadvantages of such participation? The
values are fairly obvious: activities can increase your enjoyment
of college life, provide a welcome break from study, introduce you
to a wider circle of friends, and allow you to gain skills and
awareness that can carry over into later work and leisure opportunities.

Activities can have direct applicability to future vocational
efforts. The budding journalist can work on the campus newspaper;
the business-administration major can gain experience in working on
and eventually chairing committees; future recreation leaders and
physical-education instructors can referee intramural basketball;
drafting majors can put their learning to use in stage design.
Probably the most important thing about these activities is that
they involve learning how to work with others both as leader and
follower, learning how to assume responsibility, and learning how
to function in a practical situation. Students not only satisfy
their own needs through nonacademic activities, but they can offer
services to the college community and even to the general community,
since student activities are not limited to the campus. Students
are traveling to low-income neighborhoods to tutor young children
or to direct youth activities. College students are also active in
politics at local, state, and national levels.

However, many pitfalls exist for eager student participants.
These potential problems include getting involved in too many different activities—a prime problem of freshmen; spending too much
time on activities; and not planning time correctly, so that the
student faces a choice between withdrawing from the activity or
falling far behind in his or her academic work.

To the beginning freshman, the student organizations may seem
to have little need for additional student support or may appear
to be run by a closed clique. Both of these perceptions are usually
incorrect, and most organizations are only too pleased when they

can recruit another interested and competent member. Hard-working
freshmen may find themselves quickly admitted to the inner circle.

FINANCING COLLEGE

Many college students find that financing their college career remains one of the most demanding and anxiety-producing tasks
that they are required to accomplish. Money for college comes from
a variety of sources, including contributions from parents and
other relatives, work, and personal savings. Other possibilities
that are sometimes ignored include (1) scholarships and grants,
(2) low-interest loans, (3) part-time jobs and work/study jobs,
(4) borrowing money from parents, to be paid back later on a regular basis, with or without interest, and (5) finding ways to reduce
expenditures.

Keeping a budget can also help you finance your way through
college. If you are perseverant, this is not difficult, but for
many students the task—while recognized as laudable—just can't
be done. Keeping a budget requires recording every expense and
every source of income and then categorizing each expense as being
for food, housing, social activities, health, transportation, books
and supplies, and so on. If you can do this satisfactorily, you
will find it very helpful; if you are unable to maintain adequate
records, you will have to find an alternative approach.

PHYSICAL HEALTH

American and Canadian college students are an amazingly
healthy group. Major illness is rare, and were it not for automobile accidents, other accidents, and suicide, the death rate would
be the lowest of any age group. Yet in many ways, college students
are heedless of their health and do little to maintain it.

Health professionals agree that preventive medicine and good
personal health care would reduce the rates of illness and death
to a considerable extent. For college students, this translates
into fewer classes missed, fewer exams taken with stuffed noses,
fewer occasions when sleeping in class occurs, fewer stomachaches
to interfere with studying, and fewer occasions when tempers flare
or irritation is in charge.

What are the health procedures suggested? First, maintain an
effective and well-balanced diet. The time pressures of college in
combination with other obligations often result in meals missed,
meals eaten hurriedly, and meals lacking important nutritional
qualities. Second, get adequate exercise. This becomes a particular

concern for students who have completed their physical-education requirements. Third, get sufficient sleep and other forms of relaxation. Fourth, have regular health check-ups and be aware of any symptoms that may mean something is going wrong. Fifth, avoid inappropriate medication and avoid excessive use of alcohol, tobacco, or legal drugs—and avoid dangerous illegal drugs altogether. Sixth, when tension and anxiety mount, find some way to get away from your stresses: take a mental-health day off.

Colleges can often provide you with sources of low-cost or free medical services. And some schools offer low-cost health insurance also.

MAJOR FIELDS OF CONCENTRATION

Students select major fields for many different reasons. Although most choices are based on vocational goals, some students turn to a particular major because of avocational interests, because of a favorite instructor, or because they think it will be easy. Sometimes the choice is made simply because the student is interested in the field, without a particular goal in mind.

There is no single answer to the question "When do I have to select my major?" The student who feels confident of his or her vocational goals and who recognizes the relationship between these goals and the college program, may chose a major before entering college. On the other hand, many students do not know which way they are headed vocationally. Perhaps because of pressure to declare themselves, they begin to tell people that they are majoring in something or other, but the basis for their choice is vague and inadequate. Such students may be better off postponing their final decision as long as possible.

One counselor contends that the best way to select a major is to write down a list of all courses you wish to take and another list of all professors with whom you wish to take courses. Then you devise a major that enables you to fit the greatest number of these courses and faculty members into your schedule. Although following this advice to the letter might lead to complications for some students, the idea behind it—that you should follow your interests—is a good one.

In deciding on a major, you might ask yourself these questions:

1. Will this field help me become the sort of person I
   wish to become?
2. Will it provide the satisfactions I especially desire?
3. Will it be sufficiently challenging to enable me to
   make the greatest use of my abilities?

4. Will it give me a sense of accomplishment?
5. Will it help me reach my vocational goals?
6. Will it enable me to develop my special talents?
7. Will I be able to learn what I want to learn?
8. Will I enjoy the courses I must take and be able
    to take the courses I want to take?
9. Will I be able to take courses with faculty members
    I want to get to know?

You may, of course, wish to add a few questions of your own to this list.

For some vocational fields, the undergraduate major is very important. You cannot become a nurse, a teacher, an engineer, or a laboratory technologist without certain educational requirements. Also some fields such as medicine, sociology, and law require graduate work which, in turn, requires appropriate undergraduate training. However, many jobs can be filled by people without highly specialized training and some employers prefer people with liberal-arts or general backgrounds. Jobs in sales management, police science, public administration, advertising, or journalism can be obtained by people with a variety of backgrounds.

Selecting Courses

College courses may be classified into three basic categories: general requirements, field requirements, and general electives.

General Requirements. Most colleges have general requirements that all students, regardless of their fields of concentration, must meet. Students are usually encouraged to take required courses early in their academic careers, although colleges do postpone some general requirements to later semesters or quarters. In some instances, options are offered. You can take either psychology or sociology, either literature or philosophy. Your choice can be based on any of several factors: first and most obvious, the course that provides the best instructor and the greatest interest; second, the course that is most likely to be accepted by a college you may transfer to later; third, the course that is prerequisite to advanced courses you wish to take later.

Field Requirements. Every major has field requirements. Most of these are in the department of the major, so that a physics major will take ten or more physics courses and a person studying to be a legal secretary will take a substantial number of secre-

tarial courses. Some, of course, are in outside departments. A
student majoring in romance languages might be required to take
European history; a home-economics major must take some courses in
biology or education; and a military-science student is given the
choice of courses in political science or political geography.

Most commonly, a departmental major will consist of both required courses and options. The required courses are considered so
basic to that field that all majors must take them, while the optional courses are believed to provide breadth and depth. Such
optional courses are also called "field electives."

General Electives. Aside from general requirements and major
and minor requirements, students are free to take other courses for
which they qualify. These may be additional courses in the major or
minor, courses selected because the instructor is excellent,
courses involving avocational interests, courses with practical implications, courses to serve as introductions to new areas, courses
for the expression of creative feelings, and so forth. Probably the
most important thing to remember is that these electives will offer
the best opportunity you are likely to have to follow up nonvoca-
tional interests in an academic setting. Unfortunately, most students have such busy schedules that they lack the freedom to take
many electives.

Selecting Instructors. In many instances, you have no choice
as to your instructors. Once you register for your courses, you are
arbitrarily assigned to a class or a section. Sometimes, however, a
choice is possible. Then how do you decide?

Talking with other students and recent graduates is certainly
one approach, and unofficial faculty evaluation booklets circulate
at some colleges. Students judge faculty members on criteria such
as how tough a grader they are, how interesting their lectures
are, and how many "ah's" they say per minute. Students often have
little knowledge, however, as to how well a professor knows the
field or how good his or her professional writing is. In any event,
care and discrimination should be used with student evaluations. It
isn't sufficient to know that your friend dislikes Professor B—you
need to know why. Thus, you may find that one friend dislikes a
professor because he expects a term paper; another resents his
European accent; and a third feels his lectures are too disorgan-
ized. However, two other friends of yours claim he has a good sense
of humor and gives hard, but very fair, examinations. With this information, you have a rough idea of what Professor B is like, while
a mere vote of three negatives to two positives would not have been
very enlightening. All faculty members have their followers and
their detractors.

Not surprisingly, some instructors are competent in one setting but poor in another. A good lecturer may be inadequate in a
laboratory class; a casual, friendly teacher who excels in small
classes may be terrible in a lecture hall with 800 students; an
instructor who can teach effectively in an advanced course may be
dull in a beginning course.

Counseling and Testing

As previously indicated, large universities have a variety of
services, including special counselors for foreign students, for
returning veterans, for study-methods problems, for vocational
help, and for personal and emotional disturbances. Small colleges
hire one full-time person and may draft the psychology professor
on a part-time basis.

The counseling center may sponsor a reading-improvement program or a leadership-training program; it usually maintains an extensive file of occupational information and catalogs of other
colleges. Counselors are adept at helping confused students map
out academic programs, decide whether they wish to change their
majors, or learn to live with overprotective mothers or demanding
infants.

In some instances, the counselor may obtain some initial information from the students and then refer them elsewhere. The
referral might be to a lawyer, a physician, a speech therapist, a
social worker, a minister, or a remedial-reading specialist. For
students with more serious personal and emotional problems, the
counselor might continue to see the students or might refer them
to a consulting psychiatrist or clinical psychologist.

WHAT ABOUT TRANSFERRING?

Once you have begun at a college, there are many advantages
in remaining there until you have received a degree. Not only are
you familiar with the rules and regulations, the faculty and administration, and so forth, but you might lose credits by transferring. On the other hand, many good reasons for transfer do
exist. You may decide you want a small college instead of a large
one; you may want to reduce commuting time; you may wish a less
expensive school. Or you may feel that you have picked a college
that is either too easy or too difficult.

The pros and cons of transferring in the middle of a degree
program are many, and the decision must obviously be made by each
individual in terms of his or her own unique circumstances. But

for some students, transferring is inevitable: They have finished a degree and must decide where they wish to go for a further degree.

Planning for transfer, of course should begin when college begins. Community college students who wish to transfer must be certain the courses they are taking will receive credit elsewhere, and students in four-year programs must gear their program to graduate-school admission.

Community-college students are under particular stress, since they must decide very early whether they wish to transfer to a four-year school. Some students, of course, are certain they wish to transfer and feel confident that their performance will be good enough to qualify them; their major concern is to take the courses that will satisfy the requirements of the four-year college they wish to attend, while keeping an open mind regarding other four-year institutions.

Other students know that they want a two-year program. They can ignore the admissions requirements of four-year colleges, although some students change their minds later.

The third group is in the most difficult situation. They are uncertain whether they wish to continue beyond two years. Either they are concerned that their grades will not be high enough to qualify for a four-year school or they are not sure whether their goals can be better met by a four-year program or a two-year program. The decision can be a difficult one and often calls for the help of a college counselor. Fortunately, even this decision is not irrevocable, although changes in mid-program may result in extra time needed to finish.

SUMMARY OF IMPORTANT IDEAS

1. Colleges offer a great variety of services, and it takes a while to learn where everything is on your campus.
2. Knowing about the regulations that govern your academic and nonacademic pursuits is important.
3. Participation in campus activities can add both to enjoyment and to vocational and avocational skills.
4. Selecting the correct major is an important task and should not be hurried.
5. Selecting courses requires attention both to college requirements and to your own needs and preferences.
6. It isn't necessary to remain at the same college, and it isn't necessary for your formal education to be finished when you complete the program you are now taking.

EXERCISES

I. Do You Know Your Way Around?

Find the answers to the following questions. The college catalog will have most of the answers, but you may need other sources of information.

1. What is the meaning of the grade *Incomplete*? How much time do you have to make it up? What happens if you do not take care

    of it? _____

    _____

    _____

    _____

    _____

2. How is the grade-point ratio obtained? Try to guess your final grades, and then figure out your grade-point ratio for this

    term. _____

    _____

    _____

3. What procedure must be followed for late registration?

    _____

    _____

    _____

4. What procedure do you follow to withdraw from a course? What

    sorts of deadlines are involved? _____

    _____

    _____

5. If a college regulation works a particular hardship on you,

what can you do about it? _____

_____

_____

6. What are the regulations regarding class absences? What happens if illness forces you to miss several weeks of class? How
closely do the faculty adhere to these official regulations?

_____

_____

_____

_____

7. How do you go about declaring a major? Changing a major?

_____

_____

_____

8. If you have a special project closely related to your college
program, is there any way you can get faculty supervision for

the project and receive academic credit? _____

_____

_____

9. Where on your campus can you go:

if you think you have sprained your ankle? _____

if you need to find new housing within a week? _____

if you require childcare services? _____

if you are a foreign student with a visa problem? _____

_____

if you feel you would like some spiritual or religious

guidance? _____

if you fear that recent sex relations have led to pregnancy?

_____

if you are beginning to think you might be emotionally ill?

_____

if you believe you have been discriminated against because of

your age, sex, or ethnic group? _____

10. Does your campus have a Learning Center or some comparable

    program? _____. If so, what services and mate-

    rials does it offer? _____

    _____

11. What organization on campus could you join if you were inter-
    ested in:

    agriculture _____

    business _____

    debate _____

    drama _____

    journalism _____

    creative writing _____

    gymnastics _____

    supporting the athletic teams _____

women's rights _____

your own ethnic or racial group _____

your own religious group _____

the concerns of the elderly _____

the concerns of children _____

national politics _____

school politics _____

List three additional interests and related organizations:

    a. _____

    b. _____

    c. _____

II. *Selecting Your Major*

1. What high school courses did you especially like? _____

_____

_____

2. What college courses do you wish to take in the future? _____

_____

_____

3. What kinds of nonfiction books and magazines do you like to

   read? _____

4. Assuming you had the time, what hobbies and activities would
   you participate in? What ones have you participated in during

   the past few years? _____

_____

_____

_____

_____

5. What is your present vocational goal? How certain are you of

    your choice? _____

    _____

    _____

6. What field do you think you would like to major in? Why? How

    certain are you? _____

    _____

    _____

    _____

III. *Financing College*

1. Do you anticipate having financial problems during this aca-
    demic year? During the rest of your college career?

    _____

    _____

    _____

2. Discuss each of the following in terms of its (a) present con-
    tribution and (b) potential contribution to your having enough
    money to complete college.

    Earnings _____

    _____

Savings _____

_____

Scholarships _____

_____

Loans _____

_____

Help from parents, spouse, or other relatives _____

_____

Other (be specific) _____

_____

OBJECTIVES

1. To consider the usage of time in general.

2. To help you schedule your own time by deciding how to spend the hours of the week.

3. To help you schedule your own time by deciding how to spend the days of the month.

4. To provide examples of and specific suggestions for time schedules.

Chapter 3

Planning Your Time

How much of your time is your own time? How much is mortgaged to obligations for studies, for family, for work, and for chores? Younger college students often feel that "their own time" has not yet begun, perhaps will not begin until they are settled into a job (Kastenbaum, 1966). In college, all their time is mortgaged to the pursuit of knowledge and credits, although they "steal" a little time for themselves. However, stolen time, like stolen money, is likely to arouse feelings of guilt and concern.

Many such students put in a 16-hour day. Although much or even most of the 16 hours does not involve actual school work, the feeling that "I should be studying" is so pervasive that the nonwork time may not be fully enjoyed.

Part-time students, working students, and students with family responsibilities have different concerns with time: they are often so busy that they rarely have any time to call their own. If he isn't doing school work, he is doing housework; if she isn't reading her physics, she is reading to her children. Free time seems a myth.

However, there is considerable risk in constantly postponing "your time." You may well become so frustrated with your hectic schedule that you decide to give up something important to you rather than continue for another two or four or six years without sufficient satisfaction from things you can do only during your own time. Or you may suffer "burn out," lose your zest for your activities, and begin to do a less adequate job as a result.

There needs to be a balance between time for you and time for your obligations. This balance requires that you establish priorities for yourself. You must decide which time expenditures are really important and which can be postponed or forgotten.

But you can also improve your situation in another way—by planning your use of time. Such planning takes thought and self-discipline, but it can keep time from sliding through your fingers. If your time is effectively planned, you are likely to have minutes, hours, and even days available that you can consider "your time." This time is not stolen, and it doesn't need to be earned by good behavior. It is your time without strings.

TIME IS SLIPPERY

How does time slip through your fingers?

Is this you? You have an hour between classes on Monday, Wednesday, and Friday, but somehow you never get more than 15 minutes of work done during that hour; frequently you get nothing accomplished. Or it is time to leave for home, but you spot yesterday's college newspaper on an empty chair, and you sit down and read it for 30 minutes. Or you cannot decide whether to study history, practice for speech class, or put the finishing touches on a mechanical-drawing problem, so you fiddle with each assignment before deciding there is no longer enough time to do any of them adequately. Or you find that the library book you need is out on 2-hour loan, so you chat with a friend until the book is returned.

Days and weeks slide by in the same fashion. You do not want to wait in line in the library Friday afternoon, so you do not take out the book until noon Monday. You allow yourself two weeks after the beginning of classes to "get used to things again" before bothering to open a book. You are "the kind of person who works best under pressure," so you wait until the pressure is really on. You have lots of time to read the text before the next exam; then, during the weekend, you decide to take a camping trip.

This controllable slippage of time is made worse by uncontrollable slippage. Your car breaks down, and you spend the entire day going to and from garages. You catch the flu. You spend an evening comforting a friend whose wife has just announced she wants a divorce. Your employer needs someone to work overtime, and you are coming up for a promotion soon. The person who borrowed your textbook left it at home.

And all of the loss of time is compounded by a problem common to both students and nonstudents—underestimating the length of time required to accomplish something.

An effective time schedule will help you feel secure. You'll know that sufficient time has been allocated for the tasks that must be done—and without a last-minute rush—and that enough time has been allocated for you to do the things you want to do without worrying that you should be somewhere else doing something else.

PLANNING A TIME SCHEDULE

Planning time consists of two components: planning the minutes and hours and planning the days and weeks. Planning the minutes and hours will help avoid wasting time unnecessarily (a certain amount of "goofing off" may be necessary); planning the days and weeks will help avoid last-minute cramming and all-night sieges to complete term papers and laboratory reports. In combination, both types of planning will help provide time for leisure and for non-academic concerns without sacrificing the time required to complete your studies. Because planning provides time that is truly *your* time, the academic and other obligations seem less irritating and produce less emotional pressure. *Your* time can be used as you wish —for leisure, for sleeping, for pleasure reading, for pursuing personal interests, for athletics or family activities, or for digging more deeply into an academic subject.

Planning a time schedule requires consideration of numerous factors. You need to know the hours each week over which you have little or no control—for instance, hours spent in class meetings, travel, meals, sleep, and part-time work. You also need to know about how many hours each week will be required for each course. Most importantly, you need to take an honest look at yourself.

For example, are you a "night person" or a "day person"? That is, do you do your best studying early in the morning, or are you hard put to get started before nine at night? Another question you might ask yourself is what sort of work cycle you maintain. Are you able to move ahead, perhaps slowly but nonetheless steadily? Or do you plunge ahead for a few days and then find your output reduced for a day or two?

This is not the time to condemn yourself for not being perfect or to become angry with the world because of the pressures on you. This is the time to look at the real you and the real world and to make realistic decisions about how you will allocate your time. Scheduling is easier, of course, for those who have had previous experience with college, but freshmen can make intelligent judgments based on high school experience.

In theory, most colleges assume that you will spend about three hours per week per course credit. A three-credit course will thus require about nine hours a week, probably based on three hours of classroom time and six hours of outside time. But this is theory. In practice, the variability is tremendous. For some courses, you will spend about half, or even less, of the three-hours-for-one-credit; for other courses, especially laboratory courses, you will spend four or five hours for each credit.

Do keep in mind, however, that all courses tend to require more work toward the end of the term. You might assume that you

can take 12 credits and work 20 hours a week, because most of your
courses don't require more than two-for-one (24 hours of study for
12 hours of class). This would be a heavy schedule with 12 hours of
class, 24 hours of study, and 20 hours of work. However, with two
term papers and three final exams, your school-involvement time
during the last three weeks of the term may almost double. Consider
in advance whether you can weather the storm for three weeks and
then use the week following finals to recuperate. You will learn by
experience what your endurance is.

Although individual differences in time schedules are large,
there are certain general principles of value. These suggestions
include having a proper balance of activities, scheduling study for
appropriate time intervals, allowing for breaks, and shifting kinds
of study.

Balance. A proper balance of study, social activities, family
activities, work, relaxation, spectator and participant recreation, and so forth is useful. Again, the key is to be realistic.
You need to know yourself well enough to know how much time you
will be able to spend on what activities. You may also make the
decision to finish college sooner—or to take longer—than most
other students, because of your specific needs, obligations, demands, and preferences.

Study Intervals. The length of time you can study a particular topic depends on your interest in that topic, the demands of
the course, your competence in that course, your level of fatigue,
and other factors. If you enjoy the reading assigned in Business
Administration but are bored by Introduction to Sociology, you
might schedule 50-minute sessions for the latter, but 90 minutes or
even two hours at a stretch for the former. Of course, if you are
doing poorly in sociology, you might have to spend eight hours a
week studying it, compared to four hours a week for business administration.

Breaks. Again, you need to consider yourself and your courses.
Short breaks, five or ten minutes every hour or hour-and-a-half,
are usually enough to refresh you. Longer breaks may reduce your
desire to go back to studying, and you will require additional
warmup time. Breaks are most effective if you do something completely different from what you have been doing. This is a good
time to fix a cup of coffee, make a telephone call, play with your
3-year-old son, or even do five minutes of exercise.

In the same way that you use breaks of five and ten minutes
in your daily schedule, you might try to work in breaks of one or
two full days in scheduling your weeks. Whereas the ten-minute

breaks will probably not feel like your time, these one- or two-day breaks should feel completely like your time.

Shifting. Shifting from one type of study to another frequently will have somewhat the same effect as taking a break. If you have planned to read American history for an hour, you might then plan to spend the next hour on your drawing for biology or working out the program for your computer class or practicing typing. Similarly, when you have a half-day or day or weekend of your own, consider the possibility of getting completely away from academic work.

CONSTRUCTING A TIME SCHEDULE

Before going on to the actual construction of time schedules, consider these two suggestions.

1. Be certain that you run your schedule and that it does not run you. Your schedule should provide a time structure for you, but it should not be inflexible or keep you from spur-of-the-moment activities.

2. If you are so time conscious that you look at a timepiece every few minutes in order to stay on schedule, use an alarm clock or have someone call you when its time to change activities. If necessary, remove all timepieces from your vision so that you can attend to what you are doing rather than to what time it is. Eventually you will learn how much you can do in a given time interval.

A time schedule actually consists of two parts—one for a typical week and another for the entire term. This book provides three examples of schedules—two weekly schedules and one term schedule. The weekly schedules stipulate the specific course to be studied at each time period. There will, of course, be times when you don't have anything to study (in which case the time becomes your time), times when you must study a subject other than the one scheduled, occasions when you want to do something else entirely (in which case you reschedule your study hours), and occasions when you find you have extra studying to do and must schedule it whenever you can.

Weekly Time Schedules

The first step in setting up the weekly schedule is to observe how you actually do spend your time. Use one of the forms in this book, or one like it, and jot down what you are doing each

hour. After you have done this for a week, develop your own schedule for the next week.

Make sure your time schedule coincides with reality. If your
employer increases your hours on the job or if you drop a course,
change your time schedule accordingly. If your schedule isn't
working for you and you find that you need more time to study American history, for example, and less time is needed for your carpen-
try or welding projects, then you need to adjust your schedule.

Figure 3-1 shows a weekly time schedule for a hypothetical
student, Rick Stillinger. Rick's college is on the semester system,
and he is majoring in business administration. He is taking four
three-credit courses—psychology, accounting, English, and speech—
plus a two-credit data-processing course and a one-credit physical-
education class. His accounting class takes the most time. His
speech class requires preparation time only prior to giving class
presentations, which seems to be about once a month. Data-processing comes easily to Rick, so this class takes little time. His
psychology and English classes take a little less than the hypothetical standard two-for-one time. Physical education is strictly
an activity class at this college and requires no outside work.

In addition to his specifically assigned study hours, Rick has
allocated several hours a week as *flexible* time—some during the
daytime hours when he is on campus and near the library and some
during the evening when he is normally home. These flexible hours
are to permit extra time to study for exams and work on term papers,
to compensate for time lost by illness, to reschedule time spent
in recreation, and so on.

Later in the semester, Rick might decide to spend some time
taking a swimming class at the local YMCA, joining the church youth
group, or working on the college yearbook. He obviously has considerable discretionary time: note that he has his "own time" Fridays
and Saturdays from late afternoon on, virtually all of Sunday, and
much of Tuesday and Thursday evenings. Since he lives near campus,
he doesn't have to allocate transportation time, and he isn't responsible for any family chores or housework.

Now look at the schedule itself:

1. All unchangeable hours are underlined.

2. He has scheduled early morning classes three days a week
and has work early Saturday morning, but he can still sleep late
three days a week.

3. He has avoided scheduling several hours of consecutive
classes, which permits breaks—and often study opportunities—
after most of his classes. (Studying just after a class period is
very helpful, as is a few minutes of review just prior to the class
period.

Figure 3-1.   Weekly time schedule

Name ▶ *Rick Stillingn*

Hour	Mon.	Tues.	Wed.	Thurs.	Fri.	Sat.	Sun.
7:00	BREAKFAST						SLEEP
8:00	PSYCHOLOGY	FLEXIBLE TIME	PSYCHOLOGY	FLEXIBLE TIME	PSYCHOLOGY	WORK	
9:00	STUDY PSYCH.		STUDY PSYCH.		STUDY PSYCH.		
10:00	ACCOUNTING	SPEECH	ACCOUNTING	SPEECH	ACCOUNTING LAB		CHURCH
11:00	STUDY ENGLISH		STUDY ENGLISH				BRUNCH
12:00	LUNCH				COMPLETE ACCOUNTING PROBLEMS		
1:00	STUDY ENGLISH	DATA PROCESSING	STUDY ENGLISH	DATA PROCESSING	LUNCH		OWN TIME
2:00	ENGLISH		ENGLISH		ENGLISH		
3:00	PHYS. ED.	WORK ON ACCOUNTING PROBLEMS	PHYS. ED	WORK ON DATA PROCESSING	STUDY ENGLISH		
4:00	FLEXIBLE TIME		FLEXIBLE TIME		FLEXIBLE TIME		
5:00	RELAX AND FLEXIBLE TIME				OWN TIME	OWN TIME	
6:00	DINNER						
7:00	STUDY PSYCH	OWN TIME	STUDY PSYCH	FLEXIBLE TIME			
8:00	STUDY		WORK ON ACCOUNTING PROBLEMS				
9:00	ACCOUNTING			OWN TIME			REVIEW AND OVERVIEW
10:00	FLEXIBLE TIME						
11:00	SLEEP						SLEEP

4. Two of his most difficult classes are scheduled in the morning when he is still fresh.

5. Rick has allowed himself a full hour for lunch each day, although he usually eats in half that time. He uses the rest for conversations with friends or reading the morning newspaper in the college library.

6. He has scheduled several long periods for flexible time. These time periods can be used for working on term papers or other demands that cannot easily be squeezed into 60 minutes.

Figure 3-2 shows a weekly time schedule for Ceci Rutledge, who faces a very different set of circumstances. She is in her early 30s, is divorced, and is caring for a 9-year-old son and a 6-year-old daughter. Although she receives some child support from her ex-husband, she needs to work 22 hours a week to enable the family to live adequately. She is taking only two courses, plus physical education, this quarter. However, both courses are fairly demanding—especially her literature course, which requires many hours of reading. (Note that she uses asterisks to indicate inflexible hours.)

Ceci takes care to maintain her physical and mental health—she reserves time for jogging, for meditation, and for attending meetings of a women's group. She doesn't jog every day, but she does run on the average of four times a week. Her meditation time frequently gets moved about, but she does meditate at least twice every week. Monday is a particularly draining day, so her ex-husband takes care of dinner for the children that evening. She reserves Sunday entirely for herself, although she often decides to do things with the children on that day. At dinnertime Sunday everyone is on their own; they eat leftovers, soup, cereal, or whatever they can find.

Ceci's daughter participates in an afterschool program on the days when Ceci isn't home, and her son is old enough to take care of himself. Ceci feels guilty about not spending enough time with the children, but she often watches television with them after dinner, and they sometimes spend time on weekends together.

Term Schedules

Setting up a schedule for the term is a much easier task than setting one up for the week. You can use the school calendar of events, if it provides extra room for writing in additional reminders, or you can purchase a pocket calendar or date book. Figure 3-3 on page 36, shows a schedule for a hypothetical second-quarter student, Ella Portland. Of course, this is what her calendar would look like at the end of the quarter. She wouldn't be

Figure 3-2.   Another weekly time schedule

Name ▶ *Beci Rutledge*

Hour	Mon.	Tues.	Wed.	Thurs.	Fri.	Sat.	Sun.
7:00	JOGGING / BREAKFAST	JOGGING	JOGGING	JOGGING	JOGGING	BREAKFAST	SLEEP
8:00	TRAVEL ★ / WORK ★	WORK ★	CLEAN HOUSE	WORK ★	WORK ★	WORK ★	SLEEP
9:00	★	★		★	★	★	SLEEP
10:00	★	★		★	★	★	OWN TIME
11:00	★	★		★	★	★	
12:00	TRAVEL AND LUNCH	TRAVEL AND LUNCH	TRAVEL AND LUNCH	TRAVEL AND LUNCH	TRAVEL AND LUNCH	★	
1:00	INTRO TO ★ LAW ENFORCEMENT	FLEXIBLE TIME	INTRO TO ★ LAW ENFORCEMENT	SHOPPING AND ERRANDS	OWN TIME	★	
2:00						★	
3:00	STUDY L. E.		STUDY L. E.			★	
4:00	PHYS ★ EDUC		PHYS ★ EDUC	FLEXIBLE TIME		★ / TRAVEL ★	
5:00	RELAX READ	PREPARE DINNER	TRAVEL ★ / PREPARE DINNER	PREPARE DINNER	PREPARE DINNER	PREPARE DINNER	
6:00	DINNER						
7:00	AMERICAN LITERATURE ★	CLEAN UP AND RELAX			OWN TIME		
8:00	★	MEDITATION / STUDY	WOMEN'S GROUP	MEDITATION / STUDY	OWN TIME		MEDITATION / STUDY
9:00	★	AMERICAN LITERATURE		AMERICAN LITERATURE			AMERICAN LITERATURE
10:00	TRAVEL ★		SOCIAL TIME				
11:00							

Figure 3-3.   Term schedule

Week beginning	Mon.	Tues.	Wed.	Thurs.	Fri.	Sat.	Sun.
Jan. 8	1st day of classes		babysit 5:30 Buckingham			Basketball at Gym.	
Jan. 15		Folk dancing			Last day drop classes	Dinner - Ed	Study English Quiz Lunch in City
Jan. 22	Mom-Dad Anniversary Dinner Out family	Brief Speech		Film Club	Basketball at Pavilion -George	Dinner Ed. 2 friends	
Jan. 29			Dentist 4:30		Basketball at Pavilion -friends	Early Movie Pizza charlie - 5:30	Study English Quiz
Feb. 5		Folk dancing car tune-up		Film Club	Charlie ?	MID-TERMS coming up Late - movie chas	
Feb. 12	INTRO. PUBL. HLTH EXAM	Brief Speech	HISTORY MID-TERM PSYCH EXAM		Rachel's Party 8:30 call Aunt Georgia 75 years old	Charlie evening Shopping Edna	Movie-Chas Study English Quiz
Feb. 19	Washington Birthday Holiday	Folk dancing MED. TECH. MIDTERM	Dentist again 4:30 babysit Buckingham	Film Club		School dance - Geo.?	
Feb. 26				Dan's birthday	PRE-MED Dance-Ed		Study English Quiz
Mar. 5		Folk dancing	HISTORY TERM PAPER	Film Club		Quarter end Dance Charlie	Serve for Mom's dinner party
Mar. 12		Shakespeare -George		FINAL SPEECH MED. TECH. PROJ. DUE	STAY HOME NEXT WEEK		FINALS !!!
Mar. 19	INTRO. PUBL. HLTH EXAM	Folk. dancing	HISTORY FINAL 2-5	PSYCH FINAL 9-12 MED TECH FINAL 2-5	Take off for Hooray		Skiing !!!

Name ▶ *Ella Portland*

able to fill in very much in advance, except for her academic assignments, which she has emphasized by writing in capital letters.
For a working man or woman or for part-time students, the general
construction of the term schedule is the same although the specif-
ics are different.

The difficulty with time schedules is not in making them but
in following them. Of course, they do require changes from time to
time—as circumstances change or even as your moods change—but any
shift should be in the direction of tailoring your schedule to more
directly meet your needs.

When you have a schedule that you have tested and found useful, remember that its purpose is to help you with self-discipline
by providing a guideline for you to follow. Keep your schedule
easily accessible by keeping a copy in your notebook and another on
your desk.

SUMMARY OF IMPORTANT IDEAS

1. The effective use of time is very important according to our
    contemporary value system.
2. Students must consider both the planning of minutes and hours
    and the planning of days and weeks.
3. Planning a time schedule requires consideration of numerous
    factors. Some of these factors concern an objective appraisal
    of what must be done and what hours are prescheduled; other
    factors involve such characteristics as how you pace yourself
    and whether you function better at night or during the day.
4. Optimum study intervals for any given course vary with the
    kind of material being studied and the background and inter-
    ests of the student. Probably the best study intervals for
    most courses are 60 to 90 minutes in length. After this length
    of time, a five-to-ten-minute break can be useful.
5. A written time schedule is often useful. This schedule should
    have some hours that are flexible and some that are set aside
    for whatever the student considers worthwhile.

EXERCISES

On the following pages are two weekly schedule sheets and one
term sheet. Fill out the schedules, using the first weekly sheet
for planning and the second one for your completed schedule. Then
fill out the term schedule.

Weekly Schedule Sheet

Date ▶

Name ▶

Hour	Mon.	Tues.	Wed.	Thurs.	Fri.	Sat.	Sun.
7:00							
8:00							
9:00							
10:00							
11:00							
12:00							
1:00							
2:00							

3:00	4:00	5:00	6:00	7:00	8:00	9:00	10:00	11:00

Weekly Schedule Sheet

Date ▲   Name ▲

Hour	Mon.	Tues.	Wed.	Thurs.	Fri.	Sat.	Sun.
7:00							
8:00							
9:00							
10:00							
11:00							
12:00							
1:00							
2:00							

	3:00	4:00	5:00	6:00	7:00	8:00	9:00	10:00	11:00

Term Schedule Sheet

Week beginning	Mon.	Tues.	Wed.	Thurs.	Fri.	Sat.	Sun.

OBJECTIVES

1. To show the application of motivation to effective study and to suggest specific ways to improve your own motivation.

2. To describe principles of learning as they pertain to effective study and to suggest specific ways to apply these principles.

3. To describe the most common kinds of distractions and to propose some concrete methods for coping with these distractions.

Chapter 4

Applying Psychology to Study

Psychologists have done a vast amount of research on the principles of motivation, learning, and memory. The three sections of this chapter discuss the psychological principles of motivation, learning, and concentration that have practical applications to the topic of study.

The suggestions in this chapter are like the seasonings for a recipe. Each one adds only a little bit, and, when you taste the final dish, you may not even know that some of the seasonings were used. You would still enjoy the meal even if one of the seasonings was omitted, and you will still complete college even if you don't follow all the suggestions. But your task may be a little more difficult.

Also like seasonings, you need to learn how to use each suggestion. Following the suggestions too rigidly or ignoring the suggestions may cause problems. It's also possible for the lack of one particular study condition to throw your entire academic program off. Frequently we seek some deeply personal or highly intellectual basis for academic difficulties when the answer is much more simple: the light may be so poor that your eyes become fatigued before you finish the chapter, or there may be so much noise that nothing you read sinks in.

MOTIVATION

Motivation refers to a condition in which you are activated to move toward a goal. Consistent observations have shown that this is probably the most important single characteristic of a successful student and that even high intelligence does not compensate for

45

lack of motivation. Relatively little, if any, learning can occur
without motivation. In a specific sense, motivation is required for
you to read a text, listen to a lecture, or study for an examination. In a more general sense, motivation is needed for you to be
willing to make the sacrifices that college attendance demands.

Some people assume that conditions beyond their control prevent them from being good students. They may blame home pressures,
bad luck, or other matters they feel they can do nothing about.
Other people assume that the power to be successful comes from
within themselves. The former attitude is termed *external locus of
control*; the latter *internal locus of control*. And it appears that
students who accept the responsibility for what happens to them do
better in their academic work than do those who chalk success and
failure up to matters beyond their control (Wittrock & Lumsdaine,
1977).

Your success may, to some extent, be limited by external factors, but you won't know how well you can overcome these restric-
tions unless you assume that you do indeed have the power and control to do so.

In a very real way, success is up to you. You may, indeed,
have an inadequate instructor, considerable home pressures, or poor
luck. But the question is "What are *you* going to do about these
conditions and about your motivation to succeed?"

There are a number of other reasons for low academic motivation:

1. *Some people may not see college as relevant to their important goals*. College is not for everyone, and some students have
work-related or personal goals they feel are more important than
the goals they may attain from college.

2. *Not everyone is able to settle down to college*. Some people are not mature enough to settle down to do college work; others
are amply mature but are restless and find the classroom atmosphere
too restrictive.

3. *Some students have selected the wrong college*. Sometimes
students end up at the wrong college, either because they weren't
aware of differences among colleges or because they were unable to
get into the college they should have attended. Good counseling can
often provide a satisfactory solution.

4. *Students sometimes select the wrong college program*. It's
difficult to be motivated when your courses don't seem to lead in
the appropriate direction. Changing majors, changing programs within your major, or taking general requirements and courses that interest you may help.

5. *Some people resent education in general*. After 12 or 13
years of school, some students need to do something else for a
while. Older students, who have been out of school for 10 or 20

years, may resent re-entering an institution that they perceive as
geared for younger people.

6. *Personal problems sometimes obscure all other matters.*
Sometimes personal problems interfere with the educational process
but not with other aspects of daily life. This is particularly true
for persons who are generally hostile to authority, because they
may likely turn this hostility onto educational authority.

7. *Some students are frustrated by the amount of time required by education.* Although many students enjoy the educational
process itself, others resent the process and may see it as a bar-
rier to be surmounted that stands between them and their goals.

Dealing with Motivational Difficulties

Few, if any, of us work as hard as we know we can. Instructors
are, therefore, usually correct when they say "You aren't working
to your capacity." And students are usually correct when they say
"I could do much better if I really wanted to, but I think life is
more than just books" or "I just don't have enough time to study,
with work and my family and all."

To improve your motivation, you need to have a realistic notion of what is holding you back in the first place. Only then can
you develop a reasonable way to overcome it. Or if college does not
seem relevant to your goals, you should consider leaving college
and working for a while, traveling (if you can afford it), or participating in an apprenticeship program of some sort. If you feel
you must remain in college, try to find ways to develop goals
that have meaning for you. Working toward short-term goals may be
helpful if the end goal seems to be an infinite number of years
away. Similarly, if you are in the wrong college or the wrong program, it is up to you to do something to change your status.

If your difficulties are personal—for example, not being able
to settle down or resenting authority—you may wish to reassess
your life in general. Personal counseling or psychotherapy is
sometimes useful. Or perhaps a close friend will help you by listening to your concerns and expressing his or her reactions.

And above all else, you must keep in mind that college is not
preparation for life. College *is* life. You deserve to have satisfaction and enjoyment from the moments and months right now. Certain gratifications may require postponement, but you should not
shut yourself off from pleasures.

On occasion, a person finds that what initially appears to be
low motivation is actually a physical- or mental-health problem.
If you are frequently tired or have little energy, it may well be
a sign of poor motivation but it may also be a sign of a nutri-

tional deficit, insufficient sleep, high emotional stress, or some
other health-related problem. If you have any doubts, talk with a
health or mental-health educator about your daily living habits or
see your physician for a thorough physical examination.

PRINCIPLES OF LEARNING APPLIED TO STUDY

Over the decades, psychologists and educators have conducted
a great deal of research on human learning, much of which has direct pertinance to effective study. This section will review briefly the most important generalizations to be drawn from the research
findings.

Warm-up

A baseball pitcher makes many practice pitches before he feels
ready to face a batter. In the same fashion, it takes you a little
while to warm up for studying. When you first sit down, your thinking is likely to be directed toward a dozen different topics,
ranging from the international scene to whether your chair is comfortable. If you are like most students, you fidget a bit, look at
the first page number of your assignment and the last page number
and subtract the former from the latter, check your watch, see that
your pencil is sharp enough, and perhaps read the first couple of
paragraphs over two or three times before getting caught up in the
reading.
In some instances, warm-up requires you to retrace some of
the steps from your previous study session. If you stopped in the
middle of an accounting problem or computer program, you may have
to begin again at the beginning. As a result, it is often wise to
reduce unnecessary warm-up time by planning study to end at natural
breaking points rather than strictly by the clock.

Repetition and Overlearning

You have just been introduced to three people you have never
met before. About five minutes later, you meet one of them on the
street. What are the odds that you will remember his or her name?
After a second meeting, however, you may find that the person's
name often comes into the conversation and that you share two
classes; the name and face are repeated in your experience in con-
junction with each other. All things being equal, the more repeti-

tions of the name in association with the person, the better you
learn the name and the longer you remember it.

Once you have learned something to a minimally satisfactory
level, additional repetitions will still improve learning and retard forgetting. Both football players and stage actors overlearn
their roles, so that the appropriate response comes easily and
automatically. This overlearning is accomplished by many repetitions.

You can however, reach a point of saturation or boredom with
learning particular material. When this happens, further repetitions may not be helpful.

Massed versus Distributed Practice

The term *massed practice* refers to doing most of the learning
or memorizing at one sitting, while *distributed practice* means that
the learning has occurred over a number of briefer sessions. Deciding which approach is better for academic study depends on many
factors, including motivation, the length of time for massed practice, the length of time for each session, the time between sessions of distributed practice, the need for warm-up, and so forth.

If massed-practice sessions are too long, new information is
no longer absorbed; you become saturated. If distributed-practice
sessions are too brief or too far apart, warm-up consumes too much
time and considerable forgetting occurs. Research suggests that
distributed practice leads to longer recall (Anderson, 1967), which
is consistent with what learning theorists have encouraged over the
years. However, cramming can be very useful when an exam is coming
up tomorrow and you haven't studied.

Although valid generalizations are difficult to make, it would
appear that cramming is valuable if used for review, integration,
and overlearning. It is counterproductive if cramming before an
exam represents your first real attempt to study the material or if
you are concerned with later recall.

Whole versus Part Learning

Whole learning involves learning material by going over it in
its entirety, while *part learning* involves learning a small segment well, then going on to the next segment. In memorizing a poem
by the part method, you might memorize the first four lines, then
go on to the next four, and so on. Using the whole method, you
would go over and over the entire poem until you had learned it.

Once again, it is difficult to judge which approach is better. One expert stated "the best advice seems to be to learn by using the largest units that are meaningful and within the individual's capacity" (Hovland, 1951). Sometimes the amount to be learned or memorized is so great that it becomes menacing, and subgoal rewards of finishing sections provide a needed sense of accomplishment.

The progressive-part method can be an effective compromise. This method consists of learning one segment fairly well and then going on to the next segment and learning the two together. The same steps are followed with subsequent segments. Although some overlearning takes place with the earlier parts, the progressive-part approach, in combination with using the largest possible meaningful units, is a study technique that is supported by research results. At present, evidence regarding whole versus part learning is not sufficiently conclusive to persuade anyone to give up an approach that has been found successful.

Knowledge of Results

Imagine practicing riflery without knowing whether you are hitting the target. How much improvement would you show over a period of time? Not very much, and the same difficulty prevails if you ignore returned exams and other materials. Although faculty members are not always very helpful in this matter, you can often receive permission to visit the professor's office and look over the complete examination with correct answers immediately after the tests are returned (and sometimes even before they are returned).

Transfer of Training

Positive transfer of training occurs when learning how to do one type of task will facilitate learning another task. Thus, learning to type on a small portable will make learning to use a large electric typewriter much easier. Negative transfer takes place when previous learning interferes with learning a new task. If you have spent several years using the hunt-and-peck system on the typewriter, you may have more difficulty learning the proper touch system than someone who has never typed before.

Five ways to improve learning by using positive transfer techniques have been suggested (Ellis, 1965).

1. Obtain the greatest possible similarity between the learning situation and the testing situation. If you want to learn how to answer essay questions in history, write your own essay questions and practice answering them.

2. When possible, obtain experience with the task itself. If
you are studying auto mechanics, spend some time fixing cars and
applying the principles you have learned in school to what you are
doing in the shop.

3. Look for a variety of examples when you learn concepts and
principles. You might wish to ask the instructor for concrete examples of the theories and principles being discussed.

4. Label for yourself the important features of the task.

5. Make certain that you understand basic principles rather
than isolated facts and definitions.

Rote Learning versus Meaningful Learning

Learning by rote refers to memorizing in a mechanical way,
without regard to the meaning of the material being learned. Pre-
sumably, education involves learning meaningful material, but you
may not feel that the material has any relevance to you. Memorizing
dates for history, grammatical rules for English, or lettering
styles for printing management may all seem like memorizing nonsense syllables. Hopefully, your instructor will put what you are
learning into a meaningful framework, but you yourself may need to
develop meaning associated with the material to be learned. The
more meaning you can bring to the material, the easier you will
find your study.

So far in this chapter we have focussed on what is going on
within you. Now we want to look at your physical and social environment, to consider how you are affected by what goes on around
you and how you can help create the kind of environment that will
maximize your study effectiveness.

DISTRACTING PEOPLE

Optimum concentration is required for effective study. Informal conversations can be both valuable and pleasant, but you
shouldn't have them during the time you have established for study.
This is especially true when you're in the library, where conversation may distract not only the participants but those sitting
nearby.

People who distract you can sometimes be dealt with directly.
Noisy roommates or dormmates can often be quieted by a direct request; sometimes the problem must be settled by establishing quiet
hours. If you study at home, you may need to remind family members
that the television is too loud or that effective study depends on

not being disturbed by others dropping in to talk about the day's happenings.

Sometimes the distracting person is beyond your influence—for example, a noisy neighbor or your cranky 16-month-old daughter. In these cases, you will need to readjust your study schedule, find another place to study, or learn to concentrate in spite of the noise. Finding another place to study is often the easiest solution, since the college library, the public library, or even the home or room of a friend often are available.

People don't have to make noise to be distracting. The telephone can be distracting, not only because of the ring but because of who is doing the ringing. Your best bet is to get someone else to answer the telephone and take a message for you, although your curiosity about what Jean wanted or whether Dean will call back or what you have done to deserve a personal call from Professor Kahana will sometimes make further study impossible. Nonetheless, if you have the endurance, have someone else arrange for you to call back during your next study break.

Another kind of distracting person is someone whom you like or enjoy talking to so much that simply being in the same room makes study impossible. Give yourself a test period; try studying facing away from each other and agree that you will share a cup of coffee *only* after two hours of study; do what you can. If these arrangements don't work, then you will need to spend your study time apart.

Individual differences in ability to concentrate under noisy conditions are great. Some people can read in a busy airport, while others keep looking up every few moments. Certain individuals can concentrate in spite of sitting ten feet from a blaring television set, while others are distracted by the hum of an electric typewriter. Meaningful noise, such as conversation or television, is probably more distracting than meaningless noise, such as children shouting during their play, but even the definitions of *meaningful* and *meaningless* have individual variation. For example, a student majoring in music history found that her knowledge of music made almost all classical recordings so meaningful that she was quickly distracted by even a few bars, while her husband could easily concentrate on a Russian novel or his engineering-systems journals with Bach, Brahms, or Beethoven blaring a few feet away.

It seems, then, that you should make a concerted effort to locate a quiet place for study, although you do need to be prepared to concentrate enough to ignore normal everyday activities and noises. You need to understand how much noise and distraction you personally can handle, but keep in mind that it takes energy to shut out noise and that this energy may cause you to become

fatigued more quickly. If the study area you have selected has too
many distractions, find a quieter place, even if it involves some
nuisance in getting there. Two hours of concentrated study in the
library may be worth six or eight hours of interrupted study at
home or in the dormitory.

DISTRACTING PERSONAL PROBLEMS

Tuition is going up $200 next fall, and you barely have enough
money to pay the present tuition; or your ex-wife has started going
out with your accounting professor; or your mother has just been
found to have breast cancer; or your apartment building has just
been purchased by a large real-estate firm, and all leases are
automatically cancelled.

Life is filled with an immense variety of distracting personal problems, and these problems are likely to interfere with
your ability to concentrate. In some instances, such as learning
that your mother needs surgery, you may find professorial sympathy
and permission to delay a term paper or final examination. But
even the most sympathetic instructor is unlikely to give you special concessions because your lease is cancelled or your ex-wife
is dating a faculty member.

Much of the issue is up to you. You must decide whether the
personal problem is so draining that you need to permit yourself
something extra—some time off from studying, a day hiking in the
country, or an evening with friends—or whether you have the ability to push past the problem and return to effective study. When
you are trying to read your chemistry book or work out an accounting problem, your thoughts will wander to the chemistry of cancer
or to the professor of accounting. You may need to put your book
down and spend some time concentrating on the problem, thinking
about what might happen, even jotting down some of the possible
things you might be able to do. Even though the outside pressures
are great, the decision to study or not to study is still up to
you. However, you may wish to seek counseling if the problems appear too pervasive or demanding and if you find your inability to
concentrate becomes chronic.

Sometimes the personal problems are minor, but press in on
your thinking nonetheless. In these cases, try to think the problem through logically and carefully, devoting all your intellectual energies to a clear understanding of the difficulty. If this
does not resolve the problem, make the decision to return to it
after your studies. Or if you have that gnawing feeling that not
enough time is available to complete your present task, then put
down your books and figure out how long it will probably take you.

If you really don't have enough time, you might allow a brief period for calling yourself names, but then you need to apportion the remaining time among the remaining tasks and return to your studies.

STUDY-AREA DISTRACTIONS

A number of distractions, in addition to too much noise, can occur in the study area. These include distractions due to temperature, location, furniture, and lighting.

Room Temperature

Each of us has a temperature range within which we like to function, and we undoubtedly do our best work when room temperature is within that range. There is a tendency, however, to set the thermostat too high, which is likely to cause drowsiness. It's better to feel a little cool and put on a sweater than to feel so comfortable that you become sleepy.

Location

Research has shown that using exactly the same location to study any given course is very helpful, even though it may not be possible to do *all* of your studying in the same place (Fox, 1962). A more common alternative is to have one place at home and one place on campus, usually the library, for studying. Both places should be selected with careful thought to distractions; in particular, find a place at the library where you will not be tempted to look up every few moments to respond to the movements of those around you.

Furniture

Selecting one area at home or in the dormitory for study allows you to plan the furniture for that area. Here are some suggestions:
1. Your desk should provide ample space for spreading out materials, with a surface of at least 30" × 18" (76 cm × 46 cm) and bigger if possible. Keep the surface as uncluttered as you can.
2. A bookcase next to the desk provides additional surface space with a minimum of lost floor space. In addition, it offers

a handy place for a dictionary, a thesaurus, textbooks, and so
forth, all of which are extremely helpful.

3. If possible, keep a junk drawer in your desk—a drawer
into which you can just sweep everything from the top of your desk.
You can retrieve the materials after you finish studying but be
sure to avoid the temptation of going through all those old letters,
photographs, name cards, receipts, and advertisements during the
time you have allocated for study.

4. If you frequently use a typewriter, have it on a typing
table or a surface several inches lower than your desk top. The
most comfortable arm height for typing is lower than the usual desk
height, and your arms will become fatigued much more quickly if
you have to reach up.

5. Have a straight-backed, comfortable chair that is the
proper height for both you and the desk. Studying in a chair that
is too comfortable is likely to lull you to sleep, and studying in
bed will almost certainly encourage sleep, especially if the work
you are doing is not interesting. However, certain tasks, such as
reading a novel you enjoy or trying to follow the steps of an already completed computer program, can often be done in a comfortable chair.

6. Place the desk so that it faces away from action, but
make your own judgment as to whether it should face out a window
or away from the window.

7. Your study area should be psychologically as well as
physically comfortable and psychologically as well as physically
devoid of distractions. Therefore, decorate the area in such a way
that you enjoy being there but don't display too many reminders of
people and places that might stir up lengthy reminiscences.

Lighting

The importance of proper lighting is often underestimated. The
light should be bright, but it shouldn't cause glare or reflect into your eyes. The entire room should have some light, so that your
eyes don't need to adapt to new conditions every time you look up
from your work. Indirect lighting is better than direct lighting,
and gooseneck or tensor lamps may produce too much glare.

The harmful effects of inadequate lighting, like the harmful
effects of much of what we have discussed in these past few pages,
are subtle, and you might easily be a successful student for many
years without ever realizing that your task was made more difficult
by inadequate study conditions.

SUMMARY OF IMPORTANT IDEAS

1. Little if any learning can occur without motivation.
2. Students who assume that conditions outside their control
    prevented them from being good students are less successful
    than are those who assume that they themselves are responsible
    for their performance.
3. Poor academic motivation can be caused by factors such as
    students seeing college as irrelevant to their important
    goals, students being unable to settle down, students having
    selected the wrong college or wrong course of study, or stu-
    dents having personal and attitudinal problems.
4. There are ways to overcome motivational difficulties.
5. A number of principles of learning theory can be applied to
    study effectiveness: warm-up, overlearning, boredom, massed
    versus distributed practice, whole versus part learning,
    knowledge of results, transfer of training, and rote versus
    meaningful learning.
6. People can distract you from your studying by making noise,
    by intruding on your privacy, or sometimes just by existing.
7. Personal problems can also reduce study effectiveness.
8. Distractions in the study area include room temperature,
    location, furniture, and lighting.

EXERCISES

Motivation

Write an essay titled "My Own Motivation in Attending College." In this essay, describe how your motivation has helped and/
or hindered your college progress. Discuss other motivations that
compete with the motivation to succeed in college. You can use the
discussion in this chapter as a guide, but do not restrict yourself
to these ideas.

How Do You Learn?

Find examples in your own or your friends' study experience
for the following learning principles. In each case state whether
you felt the approach was effective. Don't feel that the success
or lack of success of your experience must agree with the text.

1. **Knowledge of results**
2. **Distributed or massed practice**
3. **Meaningful or nonmeaningful learning**
4. **Rote learning**
5. **Warm-up**
6. **Whole learning or part learning**
7. **Poor motivation**

A Look around You

Answer the following questions. When you have finished, add specific suggestions for improving your study conditions. Use a separate piece of paper if necessary.

	Yes	No	Describe Conditions	Describe Remedy (or indicate why it is not possible)
1. Do people talk to you when you are trying to study? Who are they (friends, family, roommates)?				
2. Does the telephone often take you away from your study? Who is calling?				
3. Is there general commotion where you study? What kind?				
4. Do you hear a radio, phonograph, or television set during study hours? Under what conditions?				
5. Do other noises distract you? What are they?				
6. Do you have decorations on the wall in front of your study space? What are they?				
7. Are personal problems interfering with your studies? What kind?				

	Yes	No	Describe Conditions	Describe Remedy (or indicate why it is not possible)
8. Do you spend study time planning other aspects of your life? Why?				
9. Is the temperature or airiness of your room disturbing? Why?				
10. Is your school library a good place to study? Under what conditions?				
11. Is your chair too comfortable or too uncomfortable?				
12. Is your desk cluttered with unnecessary objects? What are they?				
13. Are your materials handy when you study? Where are they?				
14. Is your lighting sufficient? Does it glare?				
15. Is a bookcase near your desk? What do you have in it?				

OBJECTIVES

1. To outline some issues of functioning in the classroom.

2. To provide some general ideas about how to take notes in class, why to take notes, and what to do with notes after the class session is over.

3. To offer alternative forms for note-taking and to suggest ways to decide which one is optimum.

4. To propose specific things you can do to improve your use of notebooks for class purposes.

Chapter 5

In the Classroom

The best education, some people claim, is with the student sitting on one end of a log and the instructor on the other. Whether or not the concept is valid, we are unlikely ever to have this degree of intimacy in American higher education. If anything, the trend seems to be in the direction of larger classes and less personal contact. Freshman courses in large universities and some smaller schools may have several hundred students in one auditorium or even spread out among several rooms, with students observing the instructor on closed-circuit television.

Nonetheless, even though the students' end of the log may be piled high with people, the classroom situation still provides the major opportunity for the student to learn from the professor. This chapter begins with a brief comment on classroom participation, goes on to the importance of listening, and ends with a discussion of notes, note taking, and notebooks.

CLASSROOM PARTICIPATION

Many students have asked whether it is to their advantage to speak up in class or to agree or disagree with the instructor's comments. The answer depends on the individual instructor and the personality and approach of the student. The author recalls one professor of education who encouraged students to disagree with him in class, because he claimed that he admired dissenters. However, he usually ended up giving them lower grades because "they just don't understand what's important in education." Another professor, in philosophy, handled all questions and comments abruptly, because he did not like to be interrupted; yet his

lectures were always exciting. At another college, a young English teacher encouraged all his students to speak at any time
during his lectures, and he gave higher grades to those who spoke
up frequently, even though they did not always make good sense,
because he felt they were trying to deal with their own ideas.

   Most probably you should pay less attention to what faculty
members claim they like than to their behavior in responding to
student participation. Perhaps the main thing to keep in mind is
that the instructor is usually more concerned with the quality of
the remarks than the quantity and that other students quickly become irritated with those who consume class time by constant speaking, arguing, or harping on pet subjects.

   Comments in class are most valuable, and usually best accepted
by the other students, when they are brief and relevant and when
they add something. The ability to enter into a discussion in class
requires listening to what is being said (the agitation some students show in trying to be permitted to speak suggests that they
are ignoring everything else in their desperate effort to keep
their arms aloft). It also requires the ability to evaluate the
class situation to determine whether the time is appropriate for
speaking up. Some instructors like free discussion and encourage
interruptions, but other instructors prefer to limit class discussion.

   From time to time, an instructor will arrange for group discussions, either for the class as a whole or for small groups
called *buzz* groups (the origin of the term is not difficult to
figure out). There is more to being a productive member of a group
discussion than many people initially realize, and some individuals
with high verbal ability are not able to work well as discussion-
group members.

   Gordon (undated) has outlined some suggestions for functioning
effectively in a group-discussion situation. His thoughts hold not
only for the classroom situation but for innumerable situations in
which members of a group attempt to reach some decision that is
reasonably acceptable to all.

   A good participant succeeds in:

   1. giving information or ideas,
   2. seeking information or ideas,
   3. initiating and originating new approaches,
   4. being brief and to the point,
   5. summarizing the ideas of others,
   6. proposing a course of action or a decision without
       attempting to force it on the group,
   7. clarifying the ideas of others,

8. obtaining harmony and agreement, and
9. building on the ideas of others.

A good participant avoids:

1. monopolizing the discussion,
2. bringing in irrelevant ideas or information,
3. persisting in defending one point of view after adequate
    discussion of it,
4. using ridicule or sarcasm, and
5. manipulating the group for his or her own ends.

THE ART OF LISTENING

Listening implies a certain amount of attending—that is,
paying attention to what is going on. Look around you in a crowded
classroom. How many students are concentrating on what the instructor is saying? How many are planning their race to the cafeteria lunch line? How many are thinking about the bill for repairs
to their cars? How many are wondering whether they can get their
hair into and out of curlers between the Saturday afternoon football game and their Saturday evening date?
    The duller the professor is, the more difficult it is to lis-
ten and the easier it is to drift along wherever your thoughts
take you. But the task of eliciting your interest should not be
totally delegated to the professor. If your attitude is, "Okay,
Doc, I'm here and it's up to you to get me interested," then you
are indeed likely to have difficulty. It is up to you to find ways
of becoming interested, to find reasons to listen and attend,
rather than to hear and drift away.
    In listening, it is important to determine what is the core
of meaning, what is elaboration, what is illustrative material, and
what is irrelevant anecdote. An anecdote may, of course, provide a
telling example of an important point or it may merely represent a
recent experience of the instructor. The listener must make such
discriminations as the lecture goes on—unlike reading, you cannot
go back over the last three sentences of the professor's presentation.
    Some professors make it easy for students. They begin with a
brief resumé of their previous lecture; then they give an overview
of their talk to come; after the talk itself, they summarize the
main points. Perhaps most important, the content is neatly laid out
so that even the least attentive student can follow the lecture
point by point. Other lecturers are less kind; they meander round
and round before they light on a point, after which they give

numerous elaborations, then wander off again. At the end of the
class, they suddenly zip through the last half of their notes in
about four minutes. The listener has the task of simultaneusly
selecting the relevant comments and organizing them into coherent
notes.

Listening is an active process. The effective listener must
be alert, flexible, able to interpret, able to select, and able
to organize. An erect body posture may help, although occasional
slouching may be necessary for variety and a bit of stretching.
Making a conscious effort to pay attention is often useful; this
might be the mental counterpart of sitting erect. And while listening should involve critical evaluation, this does not include
emotional over-reaction. A freshman was failing an introductory
psychology course until her instructor suggested that she was
blotting out the ideas because she disagreed with the religious
philosophy implicit in his lectures. His comments hit home, and
she improved substantially—without altering her religious feelings. A good listener can disagree with the instructor's views
without being emotionally blocked from understanding the instructor's statements.

Listening, then, is an active process involving not only
attending to what is being said but evaluating its significance,
selecting what is important, and organizing that into a meaningful
statement.

TAKING NOTES

A few students have so developed their skills in listening and
remembering that they either don't need to take notes at all or are
at least able to wait until a class is over to write down the major
points of the lecture. However, in spite of the advantages of not
having to write and listen simultaneously, most students find lecture notes extremely useful. On the semester system, each regular
class meets for roughly 2100 minutes over a 16-week period; on the
trimester or quarter system, the time in class is almost as long,
although the total period may run fewer weeks. Even if the instructor presents only one worthwhile idea every minute, the problems of
later recall are immense

Five basic reasons may be given for keeping good class notes:
1. *To aid in studying for examinations*. If the professor's
lectures were written down, a one-semester, three-credit course
would be the equivalent of an average textbook. Try looking back at
a chapter you studied a month ago and notice how much you have already forgotten. The same forgetting is likely to occur for lectures. Students hear so many lectures and read so many books during

the course of a semester or quarter that much is inevitably forgotten. It is the chance to review class notes that appears to be
most valuable in getting high test scores (Carter & Van Matre,
1975).

   2. *To aid in understanding the professor and his or her
ideas*. Good notes enable you to see the essence of what the instructor emphasized during the course. You can also reorganize your
notes, if necessary, and read them over and contemplate their
meaning.

   3. *To aid in keeping up with the class*. A brief review before class of the previous day's notes, and a similar review after
class of notes just taken, will have many advantages. The former
provides a framework for what will be said, and the latter offers
an excellent opportunity for review.

   4. *To aid in maintaining class attention*. Taking notes helps
to sustain involvement in what is going on in class. It focuses
attention on what is being said because of the need to listen,
evaluate, select, and organize.

   5. *To serve as a future reference source*. From time to time,
students find themselves returning to their notes long after the
course is over, as a readily available source of information.

   The obvious request is "Okay, now tell me what to put down in
my notes." The answer, of course, depends upon the individual student and the particular professor, but some guidelines may be
given. First, you are likely to be told again and again *not* to use
the lecturer's words but always to take notes in your own words.
Like many *always* statements, the general idea is good, but many
exceptions exist. You will probably want to take down some definitions and other brief, cogent statements almost word for word from
the lecture. Also, there are occasions when you are taking notes at
such a rapid pace that you lack the time to give them any thought
at all. You will need to return to these notes later and you may
even need to ask the instructor to clarify some of his points, but
for the moment all you can do is scribble rapidly and try to keep
up. Once in a great while, you may be in a course where such rapid
note taking is required virtually every minute. In essence, I
would suggest that you do your best to take notes in your own words
—it is helpful for both understanding and later study—but do not
adhere rigidly to this approach.

   Second, be alert to clues given by the professor. He will provide signals such as "The three branches of American government are
the legislative, the judicial, and the executive." Or she might
say, "Nothing in the writing of George Bernard Shaw is equal to his
play *Pygmalion*." Or "I would like to evaluate the contributions of
Thomas Jefferson to the development of representative democracy."
In each instance, the instructor has given a warning that he or she

considers what is being said to be of some importance. Additional
clues are supplied through tone of voice, pauses, the amount of
time devoted to a topic, and how often a particular theme is returned to. You might also wish to jot down some of the examples and
illustrative anecdotes, since they are good clues to what the instructor thinks is important and are often easy to recall later.

Third, try to accommodate yourself to the style and pace of
the individual lecturers, and, simultaneously, look for their
underlying organization. Some speak quickly, others slowly. Some
provide immense detail, while others talk more in terms of general
ideas. Some follow the text, topic by topic, while others virtually forget they have assigned a text. Some have a tight organization,
with each idea leading logically to the next idea, while others
have a list of points to cover and do so in a casual, almost hap-
hazard fashion.

Fourth, as you become comfortable with the organization and
delivery of the instructor, try to pay more attention to your own
organization. Most lectures cover from three or four to eight or
ten major points, along with a great deal of important (and unimportant) auxiliary material. It is usually a good idea to keep your
notes brief, but remember that the clever abbreviation put down
during class may be as obscure as a Sanskrit inscription when you
try to review. Also, avoid the pitfall of taking notes only on so-
called facts and on things you do not understand or may forget;
notes should give an overview of what is said, not merely what you
do not already know.

REVIEWING AFTER CLASS

A quick review of class notes immediately following a lecture
is exceedingly valuable. It not only provides a good opportunity
for learning but permits changes and additions in the notes, as
well as allowing you to locate topics that are confusing or scrib-
bles that are undecipherable. Occasionally, students will reorganize their notes during such a review.

Probably the best single method of reviewing is to write a
brief summary paragraph or outline of the day's notes. Not only
does this necessitate going over the material, but it requires an
evaluation of what is important. It also provides a good set of
summaries for pre-examination review. Between 50 and 100 words for
a paragraph (fewer for an outline summary) is normally optimum.

On the other hand, the value of recopying notes is debatable.
If the original notes are in ink and if the organization is adequate, the time is probably better spent in reviewing, correcting,
and summarizing. There is no evidence to show that just recopying

from pencil to ink or typewriter has any learning value. If, of
course, this recopying is accompanied by careful attention and
thorough reorganization, it will have merit.

A few students make a point of exchanging notes with friends
about once a week. In this way, they learn about omissions and mistakes in their own notes, as well as obtaining a useful review for
the course.

LESWIR

The gist of the previous pages can be summarized in the acro-
nym LESWIR: Listen, Evaluate, Select, Write, Integrate, Review. The
first step, Listen, has been discussed at length earlier. The important idea is to make listening an active process. Evaluate what
is being said and then Select what is relevant and important. Put
this into notes in the Write step. As soon after class as possible,
you should look over your notes and integrate them by writing a
brief summary. Finally, a minute or two to Review both the notes
themselves and the final summary is very useful.

NOTES: ADDITIONAL CONSIDERATIONS

Films and Demonstrations

Not all classroom time is used for exclusively verbal activity. Some periods include films and other visual aids and demonstrations. However, the principles are the same, although you will
no doubt replace the Listen step above with Watch and Listen. Again,
it is necessary to attend to what is going on rather than merely
observe, and since there is often verbal material along with the
visual, the task is a little more complex. Also, you need to trans-
late what you see into words. Films and demonstrations do not sig-
nal a time for relaxation but are another form, often a more ab-
sorbing form, of classroom presentation.

Shorthand

Students who know shorthand or speed writing may decide to
apply these skills to note taking in class, but everyone can develop certain shorthand symbols. Abbreviations, such as *fem*
(female), *indp* (independent), *psych* (psychology), or *psyist*
(psychologist), will probably save time without causing later confusion. Names and places may also be abbreviated; for example, *Rev*

War (Revolutionary War), *GW* (George Washington), and *Chi* (Chicago). However, be careful when using abbreviations that can be easily confused; for instance, does *soc* stand for society or sociology? Does *aut* mean automatic, automation, automobile, or autonomy? Brief abbreviations *in the proper context* are normally useful.

Doodling

Doodling usually occurs when you are not effectively caught up in what is going on. As such, it is a warning that attention is waning and that you need some way of reviving your interest. However, some students seem to doodle regardless of how involved they are in the lecture; they do not even know they have been doodling. If you find yourself doodling, perhaps you should ask yourself whether it represents an escape from the class or an absorption in the class; then you can respond accordingly.

FORM OF NOTES

The form in which you take notes influences your organization and your subsequent ability to study from your notes. There is an obvious need to have some method of indicating the points that are major, those that are secondary, and how these relate to each other. Indeed, the quality of notes is shown to be related to scores on tests based on the materials (Fisher & Harris, 1973).

Of course, no matter what form is used, the notes should be brief and legible and should show some consistent form of organization. The form should be adaptable to the variety of lecture styles encountered in a normal college. Unfortunately, some students are so conscious of form that they lose sight of what is most important: information. Class notes are for your use and should be convenient to take, easy to read and to study, and representative of what has been said in class. If they do not follow some traditional form, it may not matter at all.

Five basic forms of lecture notes are discussed below, each with its advantages and disadvantages. You can use complete sentences or brief phrases in each case.

The Paragraph Form

Taking notes in paragraphs is undoubtedly the easiest approach but is probably the least fruitful. The notetaker continues to write the same paragraph until the topic changes, at which point he or she begins a new paragraph. The form requires very little thought but also provides very little organization. Besides, it is tiring to read solid blocks of handwriting when studying for exams.

The Sentence Form

The sentence form consists of a series of numbered statements. An outline is beginning to take shape, but organization is still minimal.

The Standard Outline Form

Most students are well drilled in the standard outline form in high school. It affords the greatest opportunity for organization but is also the most difficult form to use. The standard outline form uses Roman numerals, letters, numbers, periods, and parentheses to establish organization. The various symbols are indented differentially to increase the sense of organization. It emphasizes the major points, indicates the minor points, and suggests their relationships. However, it is frequently cumbersome to use in taking notes.

The Decimal Outline Form

The decimal outline form is a variation of the standard outline form, using a decimal system instead of the variety of symbols used in the former. It is a good method for establishing organization, but it can be awkward to use because it is unfamiliar and gets complicated. The major strength of the decimal outline form may well be for outlining term papers (see Chapter 10).

The Dash Outline Form

This method is another adaptation of the standard outline form, except that organization is established through indentation rather than the use of symbols. Each time a new statement is begun, a single dash is placed before it. Because the dash outline form lacks the complicated number-letter systems of the two previous approaches, note taking becomes simpler.

With all these approaches to choose from, a student may quite easily become confused. My personal feeling is that the paragraph form and sentence form do not permit sufficient opportunity for

organization, while the decimal outline form is unnecessarily complicated. Thus, the standard outline form and the dash outline form
offer the best approaches, although both do have limitations. Of
course, forms may be combined. The dash outline form might be used
as a base, with numbers or letters whenever appropriate, or the
standard outline form might be used for I, A, and 1, with dashes
for other indentations.

Here are examples to illustrate the five approaches described
above.

*The Paragraph Form**

Form influences organization—must have some method, show
major points, secondary, relationship between these. Paragraph
Form—easiest, poorest, write until idea changes, begin new
para. Sentence Form—numbered statements, some outline, minimal organization. Standard Outline Form—best organization,
most *difficult*; uses Rom. numerals, letters, numbers, indentation to show org. Decimal Outline Form—Like Stand. Outl. F.
only uses decimals, complicated. Dash Outline Form—adaptation SOF also, but uses dashes not symbols; good organization,
simple. Preference: Stand. Outline F and Dash Outl. F, perhaps
combine.

(As you can readily observe, this form shows organization through
the use of punctuation. However, good organization is difficult to
develop.)

The Sentence Form

1. The form of taking notes is important.
2. It provides organization by showing major points, minor
   points, their relationships to each other, and details.
3. The Paragraph Form is the easiest to use and the poorest.
4. For the Paragraph Form you write as a paragraph until the
   idea changes.
5. The Sentence Form, a little more difficult and a little
   better, is a series of numbered statements.
6. The Standard Outline Form is the best for organization
   and the most difficult to follow.
7. It uses Roman numerals, letters, numbers, and various
   types of indentation.

*The decision to use short phrases for certain sample forms
and sentences for others was made arbitrarily.

8. The Decimal Outline Form is a variation of the Standard Outline Form but is based on the decimal system.
9. It's too complex.
10. The Dash Outline Form is also a variation of the Standard Outline Form but uses dashes instead of symbols.
11. It has organization and avoids the confusion of the previous outline systems mentioned.
12. The Standard Outline Form and the Dash system are best, although you may prefer to combine forms.

(The Sentence Form uses no organization to speak of, but it is a little easier to read than the Paragraph Form.)

Standard Outline Form

I. Form of taking notes
   A. Form is important
   B. Form provides organization
       1. Major pts
       2. Minor pts
       3. Relationships between them
       4. Details

II. Comparison of forms
   A. Paragraph Form
       1. Easiest
       2. Poorest
   B. Sentence Form
       1. More difficult
       2. Better
   C. Standard Outline
       1. Best for organization
       2. Most difficult
       3. Indenting
       4. Symbols
   D. Decimal Outline
       1. Like Standard
       2. With numbers and decimals
       3. Unfamiliar and complex
   E. Dash Outline
       1. Like SOF
       2. With dashes instead of complex symbols.
           a. Fairly simply
           b. Good organization

III. Preferable: Standard or Dash or a combination

(This form shows good organization. Major points fit under minor points, and the method of indenting emphasizes this process.)

Decimal Outline Form

   1. Form of taking notes.
      1.1 Form of note taking is important.
      1.2 It provides organization.
         1.21 Organization is based on major points, minor points, the relationships between them, and details.
      1.3 Paragraph Form.
         1.31 This is the easiest to take down but the least useful.
         1.32 You write until the idea changes; then you begin a new paragraph.
      1.4 Sentence Form.
         1.41 This is more difficult but also better.
         1.42 You use a series of numbered statements.
      1.5 Standard Outline Form.
         1.51 This is the best for organization but also the most difficult to learn.
         1.52 It uses Roman numerals, letters, numbers, and indentation for its organization.
      1.6 Decimal Outline Form.
         1.61 This is similar to the Standard but uses decimals.
         1.62 It is too complex.
      1.7 Dash Outline Form.
         1.71 This is also similar to the Standard but uses dashes.
         1.72 It provides good organization.
      1.8 Recommended forms: Standard and Dash.
         1.81 These forms may be combined.

(Although this form has been used with complete sentences or long phrases, you can immediately observe the similarity between it and the Standard Outline Form. It provides a good system of organization, but many people are confused by the complexity of the form.)

Dash Outline Form

—Form of taking notes
  —important because provides organization
    —major points, minor points, relationships between them, details

—Paragraph Form
  —easiest but poorest
  —write until idea changes; begin new paragraph
—Sentence Form
  —more difficult but better
  —series of numbered statements
—Standard Outline Form
  —best for organization but most difficult
  —uses Roman numerals, letters, numbers, indentation
—Decimal Outline Form
  —like Standard but uses decimals
  —extremely complex
—Dash Outline Form
  —also like Standard but uses dashes
  —has good organization
—best: Standard or Dash
  —may combine forms

(This form is similar to the Standard Outline Form but omits the complex system of symbols. While it gains in simplicity, it does lose a little in organization by depending solely on indentation for form.)

Most important to keep in mind is that notes are to serve you. They aren't to satisfy standards established by a vaguely remembered English teacher or to be neat enough and formal enough to exhibit at a PTA meeting.

NOTEBOOKS

Good notebooks, like other study aids, show much individual variation. Approaches successful for some people may be unsuccessful for others. Nonetheless, you may find merit in the following suggestions. Try these suggested approaches for at least six or eight weeks before evaluating them, since old habits are not easily broken and time will be needed to adjust to new habits.

Physical Features

1. *Use a standard 8 1/2" × 11" notebook.* Large notebooks tend to be too bulky for carrying and for note taking, particularly on the narrow-armed chairs found in some colleges; small notebooks lead to cramped writing and much flipping of pages. Also, turning

in reports on the same size paper that the other students use will
make the instructor's task easier and help prevent loss.

2. *Use a notebook or spiral book* rather than clipboard, loose
sheets of paper, shorthand pad, yellow pad, and so forth. All the
latter are easier to lose and more likely to be damaged than the
regular notebook or spiral book.

3. *Place your name, address, and telephone number inside
each notebook.* The reason is obvious. And you might consider doing
the same in your textbooks.

ENTERING NOTES

1. *Enter the date.* It is useful for later reference and for
group study.

2. *Number each page.* This information is also handy for reference.

3. *Separate reading and lecture notes.* Reserve the first two
pages for assignments and miscellaneous notes, then begin lecture
notes. About halfway through the notebook (or notebook section),
fold down one sheet of paper. This page can be used for reading
assignments and the following pages for reading notes; the folded
sheet will help you turn directly to it.

4. *Keep each course separated from other courses.* If you
prefer one notebook, separation can be achieved by tabs or dividers;
the alternative is to use different notebooks.

5. *Try to use a pen* but also carry a pencil. Ink is easier to
read, less likely to smudge, and just as fast as a pencil for writing.

6. *Use only one side of the page for taking notes.* You will
then have the other side for comments, questions, notes to yourself,
and for the resumé of the lecture suggested earlier in this chapter.
In addition, you will have space for additional notes in case something has been omitted. For courses in mathematics, accounting,
statistics, and chemistry, and for laboratory courses, this practice allows space for computations on the blank side of the page.

7. *Use an appropriate outline form.*

8. *Indicate your own ideas.* As you take notes, you might have
made your own interpretations or added your own comments. If so,
indicate that these are your own rather than the lecturer's. The
same procedure should be used for points brought up in class discussion. Merely placing your initials by the statement is probably
sufficient.

Content

1. *Use your own words.* Try to use your own words rather than those of the lecturer as much as possible.

2. *Use emphasis marks.* A mark in the margin can designate a point that the instructor felt was particularly important, and it helps to return your attention to it later. Also, marginal markings can indicate material that is confusing or incompletely understood, to remind you to get additional explanation.

3. *Be brief but explicit.* Notes that are too sparse and notes that are too lengthy both can lead to difficulty. Experience is probably the best teacher here.

Example

Figure 5-1 contains an excerpt from a classroom lecture, an example of poor notes on the lecture, and an example of good notes on the lecture.

Figure 5-1. Good and poor notes on a lecture

Excerpt from a classroom lecture: It really does make a difference how far a student sits from the professor in a class. There are students who always come in late and sit far away from the professor. These tend to be the students who do not do very well. Of course, because they come in late, the professor feels that they probably aren't interested. Yet I had one student, a girl—she was editor of the campus newspaper and very active on campus. She came in late to one of my classes and would sit far in the back; sometimes, although not often, she would cut class. She received excellent grades in my class and in every other class. I wondered about this until I learned that she studied diligently and compensated for coming late. And, in spite of her sitting far in the back, paid close attention to what was going on in class. As a matter of fact, she sat in the back just to prove it could be done, because she didn't believe what I said about sitting in front.

As I recall, it was largely because of her that I ran a little experiment in class. Of course, it wasn't a real experiment in technical terms, but I did it just for fun and to see what would happen. The day after the examination, I passed a piece of paper around the class—I didn't have required seating in the class and there was ample chance for students to spread out in the room—and asked the students to write their names according to a seating plan. Then I divided the class into three groups; the first group consisted of the forty students sitting in the first four rows; Group B consisted of twenty students sitting in the next three rows; Group C was made up of the remaining twenty students—they spread out for at least eight to ten rows.

Sure enough, just as I figured—the first group averaged the grade of low B—; the last group, those in the back, averaged a low C—; the middle group averaged a little above a straight C. I think that proved my point.

I'd say several factors influenced this: (1) better students tend to seek out positions in the front of the class; (2) students sitting farther back have more distractions, more moving heads in front of them, more opportunity to look out the window or through open doors. I remember one student who became fascinated by a couple holding hands outside of class. He couldn't keep his eyes off them—kept looking through the window and paid no attention to class. Later I found out it was his best friend and a former girl friend—oh, well. Another reason is that students who sit in the back are often under the misapprehension that they can write letters, sleep, or daydream without being noticed. At any rate, you should try to avoid sitting in the back of a classroom, especially if the room is large. I'd say any seat in the front half is all right.

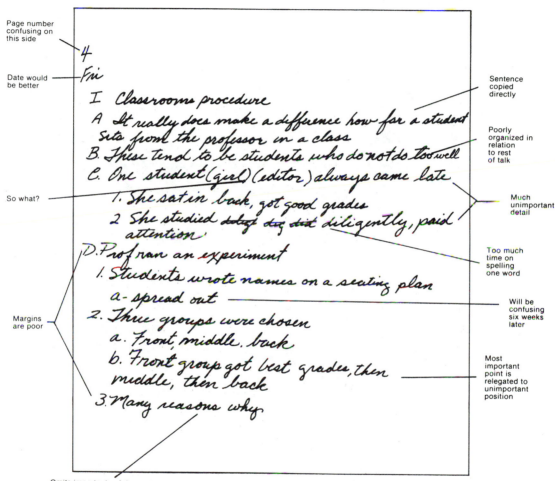

Page number confusing on this side

Date would be better

Sentence copied directly

Poorly organized in relation to rest of talk

So what?

Much unimportant detail

Too much time on spelling one word

Margins are poor

Will be confusing six weeks later

Most important point is relegated to unimportant position

Omits important points

4

Fri

I Classroom procedure

A It really does make a difference how far a student sits from the professor in a class

B. These tend to be students who do not do too well

C. One student (girl) (editor) always came late

1. She sat in back, got good grades

2 She studied diligently, paid attention.

D. Prof ran an experiment

1. Students wrote names on a seating plan

a - spread out

2. Three groups were chosen

a. Front, middle, back

b. Front group got best grades, then middle, then back

3. Many reasons why

This outline shows many obvious errors, although it does cover much that is important. The margins are poor; important points are missed. It will be difficult to read and understand this material eight or ten weeks later.

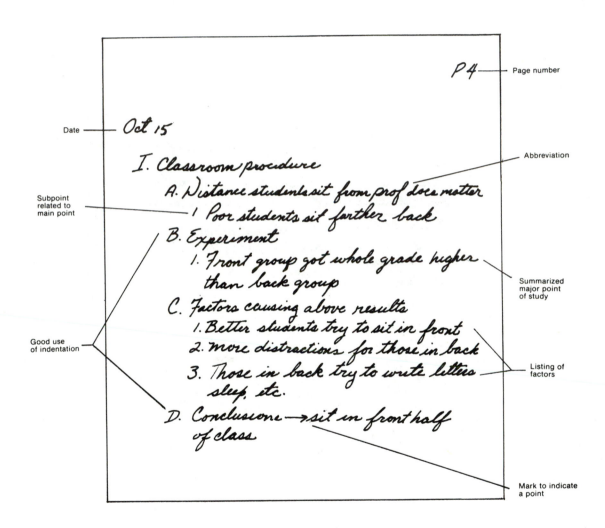

Page number

P4

Date

Oct 15

I. Classroom procedure

Abbreviation

A. Distance students sit from prof does matter

Subpoint related to main point

1 Poor students sit farther back

B. Experiment

1. Front group got whole grade higher than back group

Summarized major point of study

C. Factors causing above results

Good use of indentation

1. Better students try to sit in front

2. More distractions for those in back

3. Those in back try to write letters sleep, etc.

Listing of factors

D. Conclusions →sit in front half of class

Mark to indicate a point

SUMMARY OF IMPORTANT IDEAS

1. Participating actively in the class through discussion is normally a good idea, assuming the instructor accepts this procedure and assuming the student has something relevent to say.
2. Listening is not a passive act but demands active attention. Much of the time, we lose the meaning of what is said because we do not listen properly.
3. Keeping good class notes serves several purposes, including studying for later examinations, understanding the professor better, keeping up with the class, remaining attentive, and serving for future reference.
4. A good set of class notes can be reviewed immediately following the class period, as well as prior to the examination.
5. The steps in taking and using class notes are Listen, Evaluate, Select, Write, Integrate, and Review.
6. Several forms for the organization of note taking have been developed. These include the paragraph form, the sentence form, the standard outline form, the decimal outline form, and the dash outline form.
7. Since class notes are for the student's use and not for the instructor's evaluation, the student can select the form that is most helpful or combine two or even more forms.
8. Good notebooks, like other study aids, show much individual variation, but some basic approaches have seemed useful.

EXERCISES

I. Practice Lectures

1. Select the class that gives you the most difficulty in taking notes, and write an analysis of why you have trouble. Talk with other students in the class to see whether they are having comparable problems, but do so without telling them of your difficulties.
2. Select any course you wish, and take notes with particular care for three weeks. Then ask your instructor to evaluate your materials. Either the instructor in the course for which you are taking notes or the instructor in your study-skills course can make this evaluation.
3. Return to notes taken in a previous term, even if you must use high school materials. Evaluate these notes carefully, and turn in the original notes plus your evaluation to the instructor. Do

not hesitate to point out the good as well as the inadequate aspects of these notes.

II. *Notebooks*

Evaluate your notebook in the following fashion. First, in the right-hand column, indicate your feelings about your notebook. Place one x in the appropriate box to signify that your notebook needs improvement on the stated characteristic; place two x's if your notebook is poor; place three x's if your notebook is extremely poor. When you have finished, fold the paper so that your ratings are out of sight, and give your notebook and the rating sheet to a friend to evaluate. Repeat this procedure with a second person. One of the two raters should, if possible, be a student who is taking or has already completed this class.

Date ▶ _____   Name ▶ _____

**Notebook
evaluation**

Characteristic	Rater No. 2 ▼	Rater No. 1 ▼	You ▼
1. Proper size (8½" x 11")			
2. Spiral-type or looseleaf			
3. No doodling			
4. Notes in ink			
5. Notes on one side of paper			
6. Legible handwriting			
7. Reading and lecture notes separated			
8. Each course separated			
9. Pages numbered			
10. Notes dated			
11. Adequate outline form			
12. Proper use of indentation			
13. Subheads related to main head			
14. Avoids exact words of lecturer			
15. Uses emphasis marks			
16. Notes not too close or too spread out			
17. Avoids too many notes			
18. Avoids too few notes			

Write a brief statement on over-all adequacy.

Rater No. 1:

_____

Rater No. 2:

_____

You:

_____

OBJECTIVES

1. To describe the SQ3R (Survey, Question, Read,
    Recall, Review) method in detail.

2. To outline some specific devices for marking
    textbooks to improve later study efficiency.

3. To provide examples of SQ3R and of textbook-
    marking devices.

Chapter 6
Using
Textbooks

Learning comes through living, through other people, and through books. Of course some people can live a long time and learn very little; they can spend much time with others and learn very little; and they can read and learn very little. In this chapter, I shall suggest some approaches to improve the effectiveness of learning through books.

To be successful, an approach to reading should accomplish five goals: (1) It should help you learn efficiently—that is, the greatest amount of material in the shortest period of time with the greatest ease. (2) It should help you understand the material in a meaningful fashion and understand the purpose and viewpoint of the author. (3) It should operate to retard forgetting. (4) It should be convenient and have wide applicability to many types of texts. (5) It should be as pleasant and enjoyable as possible. Although this chapter will focus on reading for college courses, the ideas can be readily modified for all types of reading.

Since most students have had many years of experience in reading, they often feel qualified to continue their previous approaches. They may forget, however, that, although experience is frequently the best teacher, inappropriate habits may negate the advantages of experience. For example, I taught myself typing while in high school, and, for a hunt-and-peck typist, my speed was good. In my first year of college, I enrolled in a typing course, and I had more difficulty unlearning my previous methods and learning the touch system than the inexperienced students had in just learning the touch system. Negative transfer occurred (see Chapter 4), and previous inappropriate experience was not helpful; in fact, it was a definite hindrance.

Learning a new approach to reading does not require starting from scratch, but it does mean changing some old forms of behavior and acquiring some new ones. Breaking old habits is not simple, but neither is it impossible. Consider some of the common textbook-reading habits that may need breaking:

Underlining all those sentences and paragraphs that you will want to return to later but somehow never do.

Paying careful attention to every sentence, perhaps every word, but forgetting to pay attention to the meaning and implications.

Outlining every chapter thoroughly—seven or eight pages of tightly written notes for each chapter—but when the time comes for studying from them, finding it easier to reread the chapters themselves.

Avoiding the distraction of taking notes by just reading and then finding that your thoughts have wandered and the last two pages made no impression whatsoever.

THE SQ3R APPROACH TO READING

Over the years many psychologists and educators have contributed to improved methods of reading, including reading for college courses. The method to be presented here is a modification of the SQ3R approach (the letters stand for Survey, Question, Read, Recall, Review). The SQ3R method is the result of many years of careful research, experimentation, and professional experience, based on what had actually worked for students (Robinson, 1961).

STEPS IN SQ3R

Survey

A good map of the terrain to be traveled makes it much easier to follow the signs during a trip. In the same way, a good preview of the reading to be done will be helpful when it comes to the actual reading. Survey the entire book when you get it; look over the table of contents, read the preface, and skim through the pages. At this time, if any section captures your attention, it's all right to read it immediately.

Then, repeat the survey step for each chapter or section assignment. Skim the pages by very quickly reading the headings and opening sentences in each paragraph. Also read the introductory materials—perhaps the first paragraph or two—and any summary material and the closing paragraph.

Concentration is just as essential with this step as with any other. Don't assume that skimming implies paying little attention to what you are going over. Most students begin their reading with the first word of the first paragraph, ignoring all the heavier type and introductory material. Often they are not even aware of the name of the chapter, and only after two or three pages can they begin to make sense of their reading. The survey provides a kind of warm-up that can prevent this waste of time and effort.

Through surveying, you will learn what the assignment is about, what kind of organization the author presents, and what amount of time and effort is likely to be required. Five to ten minutes should be adequate for almost all surveys.

Question

Return to the beginning of the chapter, and turn the first major heading into a question. Then jot the question down in your notes (see example on page 90). For instance, the question for this section heading might be "What are the steps in SQ3R?" Always place a question mark at the end of each question, since the sight of a question mark helps provide a questioning attitude for study.

Each heading should cover roughly from one-and-a-half to about five pages of text, with a median of about three. If there are no headings, you may need to make up questions to assure that your note outline is complete. For example, "What are the major points on pages 68 through 73?" If there are too many headings, find another way to group materials—perhaps by combining two or three sections into one question. However, this procedure may be cumbersome, and you may decide to use all major headings and have more questions than are usually preferred.

An alternative to turning the heading into a question is writing down the heading itself followed by a question mark. In this instance, you are implicitly asking yourself to answer the question in terms of the major points discussed. Be careful that the questions are not too narrow in their focus, since this may encourage you to read for some specific piece of information and miss the more basic elements of the material.

Also, don't assume that the questions will tap everything of significance. Their purpose is to provide a focus and a framework—not to permit you to exclude the rest of the contents. Although you will write down only those questions developed from the major heading, it will be helpful for you to turn all headings into questions in your mind. Such questions appear to establish an active set for reading for comprehension, as well as reading to follow the author's own organization. Research has shown that students who ask

questions based on the material to be read have better recall than
those who study in the usual fashion (Fraser & Schwartz, 1975).

Read

Read the material under the heading, keeping in mind the question that you have written down. While you read, you may wish to
make marginal notations to help you later (see page 90). Reading
must be active, not passive. You will need to apply yourself and
concentrate on the book. Don't expect the book to motivate you;
it's up to you to motivate yourself. And if you don't concentrate,
you will find that virtually none of the material has stayed with
you.

Recall

After you have finished reading a section, return to your
original question and answer it without looking back to the book.
You may wish to answer by reciting softly *but audibly* (in the
initial SQ3R, this step was Recite), by writing down your answer
to the question, or both. If you can answer satisfactorily and in
your own words, then you have a basic understanding of that section and are likely to be able to recall it. If not, you have
missed some important points and should look back over the section
to remind yourself what they are. Presenting oral summaries of
text material has been found to increase retention even more effectively than does a second reading (DelGiorno, Jenkins, &
Bausell, 1974).

The Question and Recall steps, if done properly, will provide
an active set for your reading. After you have worked with this
method for a while, you will find that asking and answering questions on written material has become much easier for you. Much of
the value of SQ3R is from actually making an overt response rather
than just reading. You have been required to think through the essence of what you read and to put it into your own words, thus improving both your understanding and your memory of the material.

It is also valuable to see how much of the material you have
learned. The Recall step asks you to state the core of what you
have read without looking back at the text. If you cannot do that,
you did not absorb enough of what you read, and you should review
it.

Further, your questions and recalled answers form an excellent
summary of the material, assuming that your notes are sufficiently
brief, legible, and accurate. For a 20-page chapter, you might have

eight questions and answers, which will run between one and two handwritten pages (preferably closer to one than to two). If you feel compelled to include in your notes everything that might be important, you will later confront so many handwritten pages to study before your examination that you probably won't read beyond the first few lines.

Review

After completing a chapter in this fashion, look over your notes and reread the summary. In addition, spend a little time thinking about the meaning of what you have read. Then ask yourself the question "What was this chapter all about?" And answer the question in a brief paragraph or outline, *without* going back over your notes.

Each time you return to begin a new assignment, read these summary paragraphs as part of your warm-up. This will both add to your recall of the reading in general and help you get into the new reading more quickly.

Each of these five steps provides a valuable repetition. In the Survey step, you cover the material briefly; in the Question step, you attend to the important headings; in the Read step, you obviously familiarize yourself with the contents; in the Recall step, you force yourself to repeat the material actively; the Review step is a final repetition. And finally, you have produced a good, brief outline of the entire book that is extremely useful when studying for exams.

Initially, using SQ3R will not be convenient. You will be unlearning strongly entrenched approaches and you'll find it difficult to shift from passive reading to active reading. Also, SQ3R is more time-consuming at first, although most students save many minutes that were previously spent staring into space or reading words without meaning. Try to avoid the temptation to take short cuts, especially at the beginning. Once you are comfortable with the method and can use it easily, you can develop your own variations. In the long run, SQ3R will save considerable time by making learning more thorough and by retarding forgetting.

USING EMPHASIS MARKS

Students commonly err by marking too much in their textbooks. I have seen books with one-third or more of the sentences underlined, although this makes the review tantamount to a complete rereading. However, the proper use of emphasis marks is extremely

helpful and is one of the definite advantages in owning a book
rather than borrowing one from a friend or the library.

Each student needs to develop his or her own shorthand, of
course, but some general guidelines can be given.

1. *Underline names, dates, places, and definitions* that im-
press you as being important. You might prefer to use a red pencil,
a ball-point pen, or a felt pen to make these lines stand out even
more.

2. *Underline such words* as *first, second,* and *last* when they
point to statements worth remembering, such as "Three major categories of computer programs are . . . ." If the author doesn't
plainly indicate the three categories with numerals, you can write
your own numbers in the margin.

3. *Place parentheses around paragraphs or lengthy selections*
that you wish to return to later. Remember, however, that marking
too many is likely to cause you to ignore all of them when you review.

4. *Put a question mark in the margin* by any statements that
you don't understand. If a particular word or phrase is unclear,
draw a circle around it. You can check the meaning later, perhaps
even writing a brief explanation in the margin.

5. *Place a star or asterisk in the margin* by any selection
that interests you and about which you wish further information.

6. *Draw a line in the margin* by any statement you feel is
extremely important.

7. *Do not hesitate to make any marginal notations* that you
wish, ranging from criticisms of the author's position to noting
a point in the textbook also made frequently by the instructor.

There are certain kinds of reading that will require you to
adapt SQ3R in order to make the process work for you. These include
essays, poetry, novels, plays, mathematics, computer technology,
and so forth. Some of these are discussed in Chapter 7, and you may
wish to skip ahead and review the appropriate sections of that
chapter. You will also find certain kinds of reading that will not
fit any of the designs described in this book. When that happens,
you will need to be creative enough to develop your own procedures.

Figure 6-1, Figure 6-2, and Figure 6-3 illustrate various applications of the SQ3R study method to textbook materials. Figure
6-1 shows how you might mark a textbook during the reading stage.
Figure 6-2 indicates the use of photos, charts, and graphs. And
Figure 6-3 illustrates how SQ3R notes might look.

Figure 6-1. These pages from a textbook have been marked to illustrate the use of SQ3R markings.

— what message here?

"HE'S THAT PROFESSOR WHO TALKS ABOUT EVERYBODY DEFINING SUCCESS IN HIS OWN WAY."

FIGURE 18-1. Cartoon created by Susan Levin and Richard Kalish.

→ ok — this is success for me too

Who Finishes College?

College <u>success, defined in terms of grades or completing the degree program</u>, is related to a number of factors, including <u>measured academic ability and motivation.</u> One study (Trent & Medsker, 1967) investigated 10,000 high school graduates shortly before graduation and then again four years later. Although academic-ability test scores in high school clearly differentiated those who completed college from those who entered but dropped out, a <u>very high proportion of students in the upper third in test scores did not finish.</u> Some undoubtedly returned to school later, but the study makes clear that <u>more than academic ability is needed to</u> finish college.

✱ FACT !

Predicting success becomes even more complicated. Research at one large state university divided all entering freshman into three groups: those who returned for a second year, those who withdrew voluntarily, and those who left because of low grades. Of the three groups, the voluntary withdrawals turned out to have the highest verbal ability, while those who dropped out with low grades had the poorest verbal ability (Rossman & Kirk, 1970). This means that, according to one important factor of academic ability, the most competent students chose to withdraw. Unfortunately, we don't know whether these students finished their education at another time or in another place, nor do we know anything about their later

— why?

HIGHER
EDUCATION

331

nature of the jobs available have caused many students to wonder whether either the learning or the degree will lead them where they wish to go. Finding out that the woman driving your taxi has a doctorate in sociology or that the man waiting on your table has completed his requirements for a teaching credential is not exactly conducive to seeing a college degree as the gateway to vocational success. Student enrollment tapered off slightly in the mid-1970s, and a few colleges have had to close because of lower enrollments and rising costs.

Although there has been a reduced enrollment of what was once considered "college-age youth," other groups appear to be attending in greater numbers. Women in their 30s and 40s are coming to college to make up for the education that they missed in order to be wives and mothers; middle-aged people are returning to prepare for second careers or to supplement their earlier studies; and the elderly have been welcomed back to school, either through special programs or as regular or unclassified students. In addition, enrollment of racial and ethnic minorities continues to increase at some schools.

careful [handwritten note in margin]

① ② ③ ④ *Multiple Choice question* *Know ideas* [handwritten note in margin]

Whether these trends are temporary or permanent, whether they will influence the colleges of the future or not, whether students in the late 1970s will emphasize grades, learning, or future jobs are all unsettled questions. As you read this, you can ask yourself whether the trends noticed in the mid-1970s seem to have continued.

WHO GOES TO COLLEGE AND WHO GRADUATES?

Part of answer [handwritten note in margin]

Not everyone goes to college, and, of those who do go, not everyone graduates. Going to college is associated both with academic ability and with social class (Trent & Medsker, 1967). Social class seems to affect college attendance in several ways. Students from middle- and upper-class families have the money to go to college; their friends and relatives are going and probably assume they will also; they have already developed the value that college attendance is important; they are more likely to have attended a high school that prepared them for college; and their parents were much more likely to have encouraged them to continue their education. In essence, the basis for the motivation to attend college frequently comes from the family, and "aside from adequate intelligence, the factor most related to entrance and persistence in college is motivation . . . motivation is formed early in life, probably largely in response to parental influences and early school experiences" (Trent & Medsker, 1967).

① ② ③ ④ ⑤ *M/C question* *Know ideas* [handwritten note in margin]

A substantial number of extremely able high school students never enter college. The reasons are numerous: financial pressures, early marriage, desire for independence, lack of awareness of abilities, inadequate counseling, and a number of personality characteristics that make college seem inappropriate. A person's definition of success is also relevant, since not all people define success in the same way.

— Know these [handwritten note]
what does this mean? [handwritten note]
interesting idea [handwritten note]

Colleges and universities, once limited primarily to middle-class students recently out of high school and in full-time attendance, are increasingly providing resources for part-time students, older students, and students pursuing technical programs. This kind of student mix increases the range of educational opportunities for all those involved, with the younger people learning from the experiences of the older and the latter being stimulated by their contacts with those just having completed high school.

One investigator has viewed the mix of college students on a somewhat different basis. He begins by outlining four different kinds of students: the academics; the collegiates—those

① ② [handwritten notes at bottom]

④

know these 4 types

who like to be in college but are not really interested in intellectual achievement or ideas; the nonconformists; and the consumer-vocational students—those who wish to learn job-related skills, get their degrees, and go to work (Lewis, 1969). He found major differences among these groups as to what they saw as the purpose of college. Over half of the academic group, as opposed to less than one-fourth of the consumer-vocational group, wanted to get education, knowledge, and understanding from college as a primary goal. Conversely, nearly half of the consumer-vocational students, but only 15% of the academic and nonconformist students, saw the eventual college degree as their most important reason for attending. The collegiate students were much more likely than the others to participate in school activities and somewhat more likely to work harder for grades when they were competing with others; they were least likely to believe that an important reason for being in college was to "develop resources to become an autonomous person." Since students from each of these groupings are more likely to spend time with others from the same group, a kind of subculture develops. Thus any college is a combination of these four subcultures existing side by side, while interacting to some extent with one another (Lewis, 1969).

③ *Makes sense — be familiar*

Sounds like this school

Succeeding in College — *Author never says what success is*

Definition ?

What is college success? How is it measured? How would it be defined by each of the four groups or subcultures described above? Is success determined by high grades? Getting a degree? Learning about the world? Developing job skills? Learning how to relate to other people? Developing autonomy? Learning about yourself? The answer obviously varies from person to person. Just as the definition of a successful life varies, the definition of college success is an individual matter. What is your measure of college success? How successful have you been, according to your own definition?

And some other kinds of questions come into play. For example, how do *you* go about succeeding in college, with success defined by you? What kinds of advantages in attaining success are found by going directly from high school to college? What advantages are obtained by going to college later in life? By going full-time? By going part-time?

Other questions: To what extent can learning through books and lectures, as opposed to personal experiences, truly educate an individual? To what extent are the most important kinds of information communicated through feelings, intuition, perhaps even "vibrations?" Must you *feel* right about something for it to be valid? Does your college experience help you *feel* or does it move you away from that kind of awareness? How do these matters relate to success for you?

All of which brings us back to the major issue of what you accept as an appropriate basis for knowing. Does knowledge come through the intellect or through the feelings or a combination of the two? How can you make the most of your college experience in terms of what is relevant for you? Since college tends to emphasize intellect, you may have to work harder to make good use of what you learn if you personally emphasize feelings.

Author Opinion

I can only speak for myself in this regard, but my belief is that feelings become much more valuable when the individual has a good base of information gained through the hard work and discipline of academic learning. At the same time, the process of obtaining this academic learning should permit a person to be more aware of his feelings and to place more faith in them. ✗

CHAPTER 18

how does 330 Professor feel? More Interested in feelings, I think

Figure 6-2.   The chart, graph, and photos on these pages are from a textbook on introductory psychology. How effective is each in making its point?

FIGURE 15-7. Religion and faith help some people to have a richer old age. Photo by John G. Warford.

FIGURE 12-8. Modesty is not natural. It must be learned. Photo by John G. Warford.

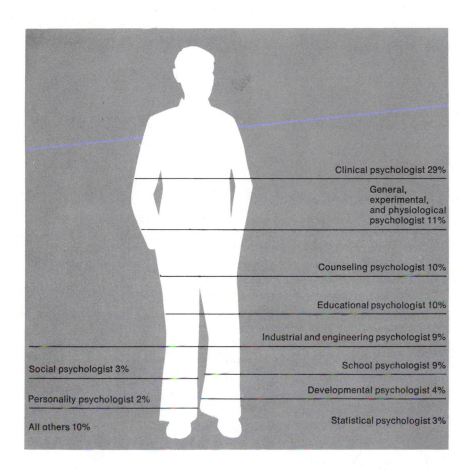

Clinical psychologist 29%

General, experimental, and physiological psychologist 11%

Counseling psychologist 10%

Educational psychologist 10%

Industrial and engineering psychologist 9%

Social psychologist 3%

School psychologist 9%

Personality psychologist 2%

Developmental psychologist 4%

All others 10%

Statistical psychologist 3%

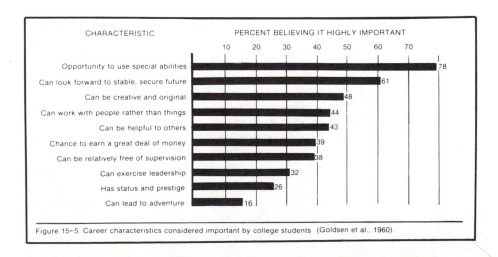

CHARACTERISTIC	PERCENT BELIEVING IT HIGHLY IMPORTANT
Opportunity to use special abilities	78
Can look forward to stable, secure future	61
Can be creative and original	48
Can work with people rather than things	44
Can be helpful to others	43
Chance to earn a great deal of money	39
Can be relatively free of supervision	38
Can exercise leadership	32
Has status and prestige	26
Can lead to adventure	16

Figure 15-5. Career characteristics considered important by college students (Goldsen et al., 1960).

Figure 6-3.   Examples of SQ3R notes for Chapter 4

Chapter Four
1. Important points in first section
   — Each study-improvement technique adds a little
     to successful study
2. How does motivation affect study?
   — Need motivation to do anything, including study
   — Success really up to individual not to outside
     forces
   — Reasons for low motivation (see book)
3. How do you deal with motivational difficulties?
   — Be realistic
   — Take responsibility for self
   — Consider changing plans to something you want
     to do more
4. How are principles of learning applied to study?
   — Warmup, spaced learning, whole versus part
     feedback, transfer training
   — Emphasis on meaningfulness
5. How do you deal with distracting people?
   — Sometimes directly — you ask them to be quiet
   — Sometimes indirectly — by moving
   — Locate quiet place one way or another
6. How do you deal with distracting personal problems?
   — Up to you again
   — Concentrate harder or put down and work on
     problem for a while
7. What are study area distractions?
   — Temperature, location, furniture, lighting

   Summary Paragraph: It's impossible to do an
effective job of studying without having adequate
motivation. If you aren't motivated, then you need to
get motivated or consider some other kind of plan.
Each person is responsible for taking care of himself
or herself and his or her own success. There are
principles of learning that can be used to help people
study; these include warm-up, spaced learning,
whole learning, feedback, transfer of training, and
meaningfulness. Distractions also need to be
handled, whether the distraction is a person, an
emotional problem, or something in the study area.

SUMMARY OF IMPORTANT IDEAS

1. A successful approach to reading should accomplish five goals: (1) it should enable the reader to learn as much as possible as quickly as possible and as easily as possible; (2) it should lead to maximum understanding; (3) it should produce maximum recall; (4) it should be convenient and applicable to many types of writing; and (5) it should be as pleasant and enjoyable as possible.
2. The SQ3R approach to reading is often successful in enabling students to improve their reading ability.
3. SQ3R refers to Survey, Question, Read, Recall, and Review— five steps in reading textbooks for comprehension.
4. SQ3R demands active reading, provides an overview, requires an overt response instead of a passive one, enables a check of recall, provides several reinforcements, and produces an outline of the book.
5. As an adjunct to SQ3R, a variety of emphasis marks should be used to indicate passages requiring additional attention.

EXERCISE

Apply SQ3R to Chapter 2 of this textbook or to some other material your instructor may distribute. If you use Chapter 2, there should be seven questions, including one that you must evolve to cover the paragraphs preceding the first main heading. Your notes should not run over 1½ handwritten pages although individual efforts will vary. Be sure to use emphasis marks. Have your instructor evaluate your work. (There are more major headings in this chapter than you will usually find.)

Apply SQ3R to other chapters of this book. Again ask your instructor to evaluate your work.

Use the SQ3R method for three weeks in one or more of your courses. Continue to have your instructor evaluate your work.

After you have used SQ3R for at least four weeks on one course, write a brief essay discussing your reactions to it and its effectiveness for you.

Keep a daily account of your experiences in using SQ3R. After one month, and again after two months, write a summary paragraph of any changes in your ability to use it, explaining why change did or did not occur.

OBJECTIVES

1. To facilitate finding purpose in your reading.

2. To describe the various kinds of reading-
   comprehension purposes.

3. To discuss reading speed and to propose
   specific suggestions for increasing speed.

4. To encourage awareness of the importance
   of building a good vocabulary.

Chapter 7

Improving Reading Skills

Students entering college soon discover that they are expected to read a great deal more than in high school. Many find this increase in required independent reading a major stumbling block in successful adjustment to college work. Fortunately most people can improve their reading ability if they are willing to make the necessary effort. Improvement in reading can mean higher grades, more reading enjoyment, and completion of assignments in less time. Few people read as efficiently as they might, and even good students can profit from an attempt to improve their reading.

Reading is—to state it as simply as possible—getting the meaning of the printed page. Effective reading involves purpose, comprehension, speed, vocabulary, and vision, as well as background and previous experience. Reading is a dynamic integration of skills, combined and recombined for each new reading task. Improving skill in any one aspect of reading will usually help improve other aspects and improve reading in general.

FINDING PURPOSE IN READING

Some people read aimlessly because they do not have their purpose clearly defined. For example, your purpose might be to fulfill a class assignment, in which case you should know why the instructor assigned this particular selection.

*This chapter was adapted from materials provided by Lawrence M. Kasdon and supplemented by Tucker Ingham.

Or your reading may be for a research report. If this is the case you should stick to the topic at hand, rather than wandering down interesting but irrelevant byways. No one can read everything, so glancing at what is not pertinent and then going on is normally best—unless, of course, you have ample time for following up new ideas.

Frequently you may be assigned reading without being told the purpose. Under such circumstances, you can evolve your own purpose and meaningfulness. For example, you might:

1. Use the SQ3R method. Basically SQ3R forces you to ask yourself questions concerning the text and to answer them through your reading.
2. Ask yourself "How does this chapter fit in with other things I have read?" This question can be followed by asking, "What are the new developments contained in this chapter?" and "What new ideas are presented?"
3. Read the material with the idea that you will tell a friend what you have learned.
4. Consider how to relate what is being read to other books and other courses. You might also try to determine how the material relates to your interests or how it might affect your life.

Evaluating the author's purpose and the significance of the work can also add interest and meaning to your reading. This may require an understanding of the author's point of view as well as the organization of material. Authors often express their purpose in a preface or their foreword, and the table of contents sometimes suggests the ways they have developed their ideas. Skimming and looking at headings and subheads further suggest authors' purposes, although it usually takes an actual reading to make their purposes clear.

You are not restricted in your evaluation of a book to the book itself. You can turn to a librarian to help you locate reviews by competent professional critics. At the same time, you can compare the author's statements with writings of other authorities and with your own knowledge and observations on the topic.

Finding a purpose in reading and being able to evaluate the purpose of the authors and the significance of their writing can add personal meaning and even a touch of excitement or challenge to reading. Reading without purpose can be frustrating and may reduce motivation, comprehension, and efficiency.

COMPREHENSION

College students are required to read so much material that they cannot possibly remember more than a portion of what they read. However, once you know what you wish to gain from your reading, you will be able to decide which of the following seven types of comprehension you want to work toward.

1. *Reading to get the main idea*. To be able to select the main idea or central thought is one of the most valuable comprehension skills and, at the same time, one of the most difficult. It requires the ability to extract the most important thought from a mass of ideas and details—to be able to distinguish between essentials and nonessentials and between major ideas and subordinate ideas or illustrative materials. This type of reading is generally used when covering the material for the first time.

The SQ3R approach (see Chapter 6) is very useful in developing this form of comprehension. SQ3R might even be extended by asking yourself, on completion of an entire chapter or even of an entire book, to recall the main theme of the selection and to write it down in one summary paragraph.

2. *Reading to note details*. After mastering the basic, important ideas, you have a skeleton on which details will fit. Details should be seen in relation to the main concepts that they help develop, not as a series of isolated bits of information. Details serve numerous functions: they provide concrete examples to make a generalization more meaningful; they provide evidence to support a conclusion; they illustrate ways in which an idea can be applied; they may also mark the limits of an idea.

3. *Reading to follow a sequence of events*. The reader of a novel must be able to keep the sequence of the plot straight. In the same fashion, a person reading history or biography must be able to recognize the chronological order of events, even if the book skips around in time.

4. *Reading to follow directions*. Skill in following directions is closely related to skill in following a sequence of events. Certain subjects require considerable use of this skill. In a mathematics or programming book, the author will usually explain the importance of a process. Then, he or she will generally explain how to perform the process, after which an illustration of this explanation is presented. It is useful for you to check your own mastery of the process by working the example that the author provides; if you run into trouble, you can glance back at the directions.

5. *Reading to evaluate*. Try to adopt an inquiring attitude. Ask yourself whether what you are reading agrees with what you already know about the subject or with what the instructor has said. If not, then stop and take stock to find out where the discrepancy

is. You might also discuss the issue with a classmate or the instructor. If you cannot see beyond the information presented, you
need to learn to evaluate and to think critically as you read. Draw
on your own experience and that of various authorities to evaluate
the author's logic and accuracy. At the same time, of course, you
need to recognize limitations in your own knowledge and be willing
to read with an open mind.

Part of evaluating is learning the source for the material.
In reading about the success of a revolutionary movement in a foreign country, you need to know whether the article was based on information supplied by the government in power or the people repre-
senting the revolution. An article about the real-estate industry,
the Federal Trade Commission, or the Boston Red Sox will differ
greatly as a result of the biases of the authors or of the authors'
major sources, and you can often learn that the author is a realtor,
a member of the Federal Trade Commission, or the public relations
director of the Red Sox. Newspaper editorials and most individual
columnists also have identifiable and consistent biases.

6. *Reading to draw correct inferences.* An effective reader
not only needs to understand the literal meaning of the words on
the printed page but also needs to grasp the implicit meaning in
the words. Robert Herrick's meaning in the following lines from his
poem "To the Virgins to Make Much of Time" eludes a literal-minded
examination.

Gather ye rosebuds while ye may,
  Old time is still a-flying,
And this same flower that smiles today
  Tomorrow will be dying.

What inferences do you draw from the suggestion that you
"gather rosebuds"? What hints are contained in the title of the
poem? What does the poem say about life and death?

7. *Reading to gain mental images.* Using mental imagery is one
way of testing your understanding of what the author is saying. For
example, in reading about an improvement in farm machinery, can you
visualize the machine in actual operation? You might check your
mental images with illustrations and diagrams in the text as well as
with verbal descriptions.

As you read fiction, can you "see" the events take place in
your mind's eye? In a course in stage lighting, can you "see" the
colors change on the stage and the effects this change will have
upon the set and the actors? Do you "hear" the music when you look
at a musical score? Do you "see" the finished product after looking
at a blueprint? These are examples of highly sophisticated mental
imagery. The more vivid the picture or auditory image you have, the

more likely it is that you understand the words of the author.
(See Chapter 11 for further discussion of studying nontextbooks.)

READING SPEED

Unfortunately some people believe that reading improvement is
synonymous with increasing their reading speed. However, reading
speed cannot be effectively improved if you have difficulty recognizing new words, do not have an adequate vocabulary, or have difficulty understanding what you read. These are some of the main reasons why speed-reading courses do not help everyone. Apparently the
people who should enroll in a course emphasizing speed are those
who already have a good vocabulary and adequate comprehension.

Varying Speed to Fit the Occasion

People who comprehend efficiently are able to adjust their
reading speed in terms both of the difficulty of the material for
them and of their purpose in reading. Some people read everything
at roughly the same rate, without knowing when they should slow
down or speed up. However, there is no one best rate of reading,
except in terms of the individual and his or her materials.
One authority suggested that reading speed be changed according to the following purposes (Harris, 1956). Read slowly when you
wish to:

1. master content, including details,
2. evaluate the quality of material,
3. follow directions,
4. solve a problem,
5. read poetry, or
6. judge literary merit.

A medium speed is used when you want to:

7. read highly technical material such as mathematics,
8. answer specific questions,
9. note details,
10. grasp the relationships of details to main ideas, or
11. read material of medium difficulty.

And you will read rapidly in order to:

    12.   review familiar material,
    13.   read to get the main idea or central thought, or
    14.   read a story for its plot, such as a fast-moving
          short story.

There is a fourth general speed in reading: skimming. Skimming is suggested when you hope to:

    15.   locate a reference,
    16.   locate new material,
    17.   answer a specific question, or
    18.   get the general idea of a selection

Skimming should be done at a rate of at least 500 words a minute, and a skillful reader should be able to skim at a rate of over 1,000 words a minute.

Causes of Slow Reading and Some Remedies

You may wonder how rapidly you should be reading. The figure of 350 words a minute as the normal reading rate of college students offers only an approximate idea of the speed at which the "average" student should read a textbook (Strang, McCullough, & Traxler, 1967). Almost everyone can profit from learning ways to increase reading speed. Of course, if the problem involves vocabulary or comprehension, improvement in these areas will generally result in an automatic increase in reading speed. However, there are reading problems that affect speed in particular. The following causes are particularly prevalent:

1. *Reading word by word, syllable by syllable, or letter by letter.* Some simple techniques may help overcome these difficulties. Type common phrases on 3 × 5 cards and see how rapidly you can say them. Then have a friend move a blank card along a line of type as you read aloud—have your friend cover part of the line unexpectedly (except for the first three words) and see how much of the covered part you can recite. Repeat this procedure. If these techniques do not help after six or eight practice sessions of approximately 15 minutes each, you may wish to consult a reading specialist.

2. *Slowness in word recognition.* This may also be dealt with in the ways suggested above.

3. *Vocalizing.* One suggested aid here is to put your finger on your lips or on your larynx (Adam's apple) to check whether you

are moving your lips or throat muscles. If so, try to force yourself to stop. On the other hand, when reading extremely difficult material, vocalizing may be helpful.

    4. *Difficulty in going from the end of one line to the beginning of the next*. If this is a problem, you might try typing a paragraph triple space and connecting the end of each line to the beginning of the next with a dotted line. Now read this paragraph several times as rapidly as possible. Again, if six or eight sessions do not help, you may wish to talk with an expert.

    5. *Excessive looking back*. Although a certain amount of looking back is done by the best readers, some people find themselves doing this too frequently. Excessive looking back may signify that you are reading material that is too difficult; that you are reading at the wrong speed; that there are inaccuracies in your word recognition and meaning; or that you have visual problems, inadequate concentration, or just plan bad habits. If you can figure out the cause of your problem, you will know what to do about it. If the reasons escape your analysis, a reading specialist can probably help you. Of course, if you have a vision problem, your reading may well be affected. Occasionally all that is needed to turn a poor reader into a good one is to correct these defects through eyeglasses or other treatment. In other instances, poor eyesight leads to fatigue, to misreading, to eyestrain, and to headaches—all of which work against effective study. A thorough eye examination is usually worthwhile.

    6. *Holding the book improperly*. Holding a book at right angles to your line of vision improves reading efficiency. This is not an old wives' tale but is based on scientific evidence. One study found that turning a book 45° to the right or left reduced reading speed by 50% and that tilting the book back the same amount reduced reading speed even more (Tinker, 1956).

Techniques for Increasing Reading Speed

    Probably the simplest way to increase your speed is to time yourself as you read an assignment and keep a record of your reading rate. Divide the page of a notebook into columns as indicated:

Date	Time spent reading	Nature of assignment	Number of words	Speed (wpm)

Reading speed (words per minute) is, of course, determined by dividing the number of minutes spent into the number of words (estimated) read.

A separate page should be kept for each subject, and comparisons should be made only when taking the nature of the assignment into consideration. By keeping careful track of your reading time for homework and other reading, your reading speed should increase substantially in as little as ten weeks.

Another technique for improving reading speed is to move a card under the line you are reading so that the card moves down at a comfortable rate. Then, start moving the card a *little* faster—not too much—each day. Here again, keeping a record is very useful. Ten minutes' practice twice a week will yield large dividends in increased reading speed in one semester. Eventually you may wish to eliminate the card and just move your hand rapidly along the line.

Sometimes a student requires help to eliminate reading faults. Many colleges have reading clinics where experts and modern equipment can offer help. Students with reading problems should not hesitate to seek such aid. Even the application of a few simple techniques for one week can increase reading speed to some extent.

VOCABULARY

Knowledge of word meanings is fundamental to skill in reading, and a large vocabulary is basic to reading success. The beginning college student often feels deluged with new words, many of them jargon in a technical language.

Listed below are several techniques that have been found successful in increasing vocabulary. Your course instructor and your English professor undoubtedly have additional thoughts.

1. *Take a tip from the professor's lectures*. Frequently the professor will define key terms in the lecture. Recording these terms in a notebook, either with regular class notes or separately, will aid in learning them. Of course, there will be many other terms that are not defined in the lectures that you will be expected to learn on your own.

2. *Keep a notebook*. It is useful to record new words—from all sources—in a notebook. Record those words that are unfamiliar to you, those whose meanings are vague or fuzzy when you think about them, and those that are familiar but seem to be used in a new way. For example, the word "class" is undoubtedly familiar to most students, but in a sociology course "class" no longer means "A group of persons or things of the same kind, or a group of pupils taught together"; rather it means "a group of individuals

ranked together as possessing common characteristics or having the same status."

A useful notebook contains more than a list of words. It should include the word itself, a sentence or phrase in which the word is used, the phonetic spelling (if you aren't certain of pronunciation), and a dictionary definition, sometimes also available in a glossary in the back of the text. The notebook will then look something like this:

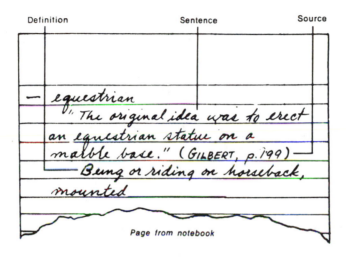

Page from notebook

The final check is to substitute the definition in the original phrase or sentence. In some instances, it may mean rewording the sentence slightly.

3. *Use the words*. In order to achieve effective mastery over the new words, you need to use them whenever appropriate, both in writing and in speaking. The more often the word is used, the more familiar it will become. After developing an awareness of a new word, you often find that you seem to come across it in many places. To help yourself with this task, concentrate on words for which you have an immediate use rather than on those unrelated to what you are doing.

4. *Study words*. In one study of factors underlying the reading difficulties of college students, poorer readers were found to have "a general vocabulary deficiency that is aggravated by a definite lack of knowledge about prefixes and suffixes" (Holmes, 1954). Is this one of your difficulties? The following list of prefixes is based on an analysis of 20,000 words taken from a list prepared for another purpose. Five thousand had prefixes and the following 15 prefixes accounted for 82% of these 5000 (Blair, 1956).

Prefix	*Meaning*	*Frequency*
com	*with*	*500*
re	*back*	*457*
ad	*to*	*433*
un	*not*	*378*
in	*into*	*336*
in	*not*	*317*
dis	*apart*	*299*
ex	*out*	*286*
de	*from*	*282*
en	*in*	*182*
pro	*in front of*	*146*
pre	*before*	*127*
sub	*under*	*112*
be	*by*	*111*
ab	*from*	*98*

Notice that some prefixes have more than one meaning. As you gain familiarity with words, you will be able to select the appropriate meaning. This list, of course, is only a starting point; you may wish to make a list of other prefixes that occur frequently in the words listed in your vocabulary notebook.

Suffixes also affect word meanings. Thus we find differences between "synthesis" and "synthesize," between "dependent" and "dependency." Often a little word detective work will provide the meaning of a seemingly unknown term.

Of course, the fundamental part of any word is its root. The root of a word is the uncompounded word or element without a prefix or suffix. When you look up words in the dictionary, you will notice that many words come from the same Latin or Greek root. Familiarity with these root words will help you unlock many meanings. The following ten Latin and two Greek words enter into the construction of at least 2500 English words (Smith, 1949):

Ten *Latin verbs*	*Definition*	*English examples*
facere	*to make or do*	*facile, manufacture, fact*
ducere	*to lead*	*educate, abduct, seduce, aqueduct*
tendere	*to stretch*	*extend, intend, pretend*
plicare	*to fold*	*supplicate, duplex*
specere	*to look, behold*	*aspect, specimen, suspect*

Ten Latin verbs	Definition	English examples
ponere	to place, put	postpone, opponent
tenere	to hold, have	tenacious, untenable, detain
capere	to take, seize	captivate, intercept, precept
ferre	to bear, produce	fertile, refer, transfer
mittere	to send	submit, remiss, transmitter

Two Greek words	Definition	English examples
logos	word, speech, reason	logic, logarithm, philology
grapho	write	graphite, graphic, telegraph

As an exercise, you might try taking a well-known root and seeing how many words you can make from it. For example, the Latin root "jacio" is found in "abject," "dejected," "eject," "inject," "interject," "object," "objection," and many more words.

    5. *Use context clues*. Frequently the meaning of words can be derived from the context. You might not know the meaning of "rationalize," but could figure it out from the following sentence: "He was unable to rationalize his failures because there was no way he could excuse them to himself."

    6. *Take an active interest in words*. Words can be interesting. For example, there are regional differences in language: In the East there are "expressways," and in the West there are "freeways." Some words describe the new scientific era: "programming," "satellite," and "clone." Other words have been created to describe products: "Coke" and "Kleenex." The origins of words often add enjoyment to the process of building a vocabulary. For instance, where did these words come from: "hoosegow," "gesundheit," "psychology"? Be a word detective by noticing words and phrases that are not listed in the dictionary or words that are used primarily by certain groups—for example, "soul," "wahine," "high," "holistic," "Chicano," and "mensch." What are the origins of these words? Have their meanings changed over the years?

    Two reference books are invaluable: the dictionary and the thesaurus. You are undoubtedly familiar with the dictionary and probably already own one. If not, you should purchase a good one.

Ask your instructor or a knowledgeable person at your college or local bookstore for a recommendation. You may not be as familiar with the thesaurus, which is a book of synonyms or word equivalents, but this is also an important tool for college.

Whatever your future work will be, it will require some reading; whatever your preferred hobbies and leisure activities are, they will involve some reading. There are few, if any, skills that are more in demand for vocational success and personal satisfaction than the ability to read.

SUMMARY OF IMPORTANT IDEAS

1. Effective reading incorporates purpose, comprehension, speed, vocabulary, and vision.
2. When you do not really understand the purpose of your reading, you may read aimlessly.
3. You can read for several different types of comprehension. These include reading to get the main idea, to note details, to follow a sequence of events, to follow directions, to evaluate, to draw correct inferences, and to gain mental images.
4. Improved reading speed is partly the result of good comprehension.
5. In effective reading, the speed must be varied to fit the occasion. That is, you read at a different speed to solve a problem than you do to get the main idea of a plot; reading technical material differs from reading a novel.
6. Slow reading has many causes. Some of the more common include reading word by word, not recognizing words quickly, vocalizing, slowness in moving from the end of one line to the beginning of the next, excessive looking back, and holding the book improperly.
7. Having a large vocabulary is basic to reading success. Keeping a notebook of new words is only one of several ways to build vocabulary.
8. Knowledge of prefixes and suffixes will help improve reading skills and vocabulary.

EXERCISES

Reading Speed and Comprehension Evaluation

In the lefthand column is a list of types of reading you are likely to do. Indicate in the center and righthand columns the type of comprehension called for and the type of reading speed required. Look back through the chapter for the categories, if you need to.

Type of reading	Type of comprehension	Reading speed
Sports section of newspaper		
Novel assigned by professor		
Time or *Newsweek* magazine		
Article in a technical magazine		
Psychology text early in semester		
Psychology text night before exam		
Review of movie		
History textbook		
Editorial in campus newspaper		
Chapter 6 of this book		

How Fast Do You Read?

   Obtain two books—one a textbook for a course such as history,
philosophy, or psychology and the other a novel you will enjoy
reading. Keep track of your reading speeds on the following time
chart. Record only periods in which you were not interrupted. Continue as long as your instructor suggests.
   Or, as an alternative, ask the instructor to assign chapters
in this book and follow the same steps. This way all students will
be able to compare their speeds.

Novel: _____

Approximate number of words on each page: _____

Date	Time spent in reading	Number of pages	Number of words	Words per minute

Textbook: _____

Approximate number of words on each page: _____

Date	Time spent in reading	Number of pages	Number of words	Words per minute

OBJECTIVES

1. To describe the types of classroom examinations.

2. To encourage appropriate preparation for examinations, and to outline specific procedures for improving efficiency in studying for exams.

3. To discuss improving personal functioning during the examination itself.

4. To provide examples of good and poor answers to examination questions.

Chapter 8

Taking Examinations

Examinations probably cause more anger, anxiety, fear, and complaints than any other academic aspect of college life. Students feel the pressure of competition for grades—no matter how reassuring the instructor may be—and they face both the hard work preceding an examination and the uncertainty that occurs until an examination is finally graded and returned. In some cases, the unhappiness only begins when the exam is returned. And no matter what their grades are, most students seem to find something to complain about for each exam. Nor are the faculty any happier about giving exams. In addition to the extra work of preparing and grading them, instructors know they must brace themselves for the coming avalanche of protest that occurs when the students see their papers.

Course examinations have four primary purposes: (1) to enable the instructors to evaluate the students, (2) to enable the instructors to evaluate their own effectiveness, (3) to enable the students to evaluate their progress, and (4) to motivate the students to study.

There is no need to catalog the shortcomings of classroom examinations; they are well known. Unfortunately some of the advantages are ignored. Studying for an examination (1) requires you to give considerably more thought to the course material than you otherwise might; (2) requires you to integrate the text material with the lectures for a broader understanding; (3) requires you to function without the support of books or notes (except in open-book exams) and thus provides an indication of how much of the course content you have actually absorbed; and (4) helps you to determine your areas of strength and weakness and to spot points on which you are confused.

ATTITUDES TOWARD EXAMINATIONS

Attitudes toward a particular examination, or toward examinations in general, may play an important role in your performance. Many students are tense before taking an examination, since exams and grades are the most visible and most talked-about measures of college success. Highly anxious students are less likely to do well when they are under great stress, and a classroom exam can certainly produce that stress.

Obviously the better prepared you are, the less you have to worry about, although some students worry about exams no matter how well prepared they are. They may worry because success or failure on the examination has broad implications, such as satisfying the demands of parents or their own demands upon themselves. Being relaxed—but not overconfident, of course—is a great advantage in taking a test, and the best way for most people to relax is to feel they know their material. An additional aid in relaxing is being fully rested and having eaten properly. Students who spend most of the previous night drinking coffee, smoking cigarettes, and poring over books are likely to feel tense and restless when they take the exam.

TYPES OF EXAMINATIONS

Examinations can be categorized in many different ways. There are open-book exams and closed-book exams, take-home exams and in-class exams, nationally standardized exams and locally constructed exams, verbal exams and performance exams, essay exams and objective exams.

Open-Book Exams and Closed-Book Exams. Occasionally an instructor allows students to bring their previous tests and class notes to an examination. Many students dislike open-book exams because the questions are likely to be broader and to require more writing than questions on closed-book exams and because time limitations often do not permit much skimming through the book looking for a particular passage. Some students who do well on regular examinations have less success with open-book exams, perhaps because of overconfidence. In any event, open-book examinations do not reduce over-all study time and effort; they are intended to rechannel students' energy from simply memorizing material to gaining a broader and deeper understanding of the material.

Take-Home Exams versus In-Class Exams. A take-home exam allows you to take the test at a time and place of your own choosing;

also, it usually allows you as much time as you need. Frequently, a take-home exam is combined with an open-book exam. It might seem at first glance that take-home exams would be easier than regular exams, but they are actually more demanding. You may be given ten days or two weeks in which to return the exam; thus you may have considerable difficulty deciding how much time to allocate to it. If it is a take-home, as well as an open-book, exam, the answers may require a great deal of reading.

Both open-book and take-home examinations can provide excellent opportunities to learn, but they may also lure the unsophisticated student into overconfidence.

Nationally Standardized Exams versus Locally Constructed Exams. Although students rarely take nationally standardized exams as part of the classroom routine, they do take them as part of a college-entrance or job-placement battery. A nationally standardized examination permits you to compare your score with the scores of thousands of others around the country. Through such an exam, you might learn that your mechanical ability is better than 74% of all male high school seniors.

Verbal Exams versus Performance Exams. Most classroom examinations are verbal: that is, they depend on words. However, once in a while an instructor will give a performance test. In such classes as typing or drafting, the exam may measure how well you perform the actual tasks involved in typing or in drawing. Other examples include a science professor who asks you to conduct an experiment and a home-economics instructor who asks you to prepare a meal.

Essay Exams versus Objective Exams. Although we can classify most exam questions as either objective items or essay questions, each of these major categories is made up of several subcategories. Objective exams are usually considered those in which the answers can be given in one or two words or a brief sentence or by indicating which of two or more alternatives is correct. The questions in an objective exam are based on the premise that there is one correct answer, with other answers being either wrong or at least less correct. Objective tests tend to measure breadth of knowledge, rather than depth.

Essay-test questions require writing at least a couple of sentences and perhaps as much as several pages. The premise underlying essay questions is that there are many ways of answering correctly and that the grading must be somewhat subjective. Essay scores, of course, also reflect the ability of the student to write effectively and to integrate ideas.

You may hear that objective tests do not demand as much study
because they are essentially recognition tests. Whether this is
true depends more on the person making up the exam than on the
type of exam. In any event, most instructors will advise you that
the amount of study necessary and the approach to study are determined by course content and the ideas of the instructor, not by
the type of test used.

PREPARING FOR EXAMINATIONS

Studying for examinations is a constant process; it does not
begin a few days before the examination. A certain amount of time
for review might be allocated each week (see Chapter 3). Group
study sessions, described below, are most effective when carried
out during the entire semester. Following a study schedule prevents
falling behind, and good notes provide clear, concise, and readable
material from which to study. Of course, this final study should
involve review and integration, not initial reading.

As an examination period or a single exam draws near, some of
the flexible hours in your schedule might well be rescheduled for
extra study and review. The student who has fallen seriously behind—and this refers to almost all of us at one time or another—
may even need to reduce the hours allocated to *own time* in order
to have enough time to study for exams *without* ignoring other academic and nonacademic responsibilities. Since classes are usually
cancelled during the final-exam period, you will probably need to
construct an entirely new time schedule for this period.

Some students find final-exam week the easiest time of the
year (not the most relaxed, but the easiest). They have turned
their papers in on time, have kept up-to-date with their reading,
and have discharged their other responsibilities in a reasonably
orderly way. These students face only some reviewing, perhaps a
little group study, and a very few hours spent actually taking
the exams. By the time the exam week is half over, they may have
only one or two obligations remaining. Too many students, however,
have not kept up; during exam week they are harried and rushed,
with term papers and finals competing for time and attention.

Much that has been stated previously in this book is pertinent to examinations. That is, in preparing for an examination,
the SQ3R notes become very useful; study conditions become important; time schedules require more attention and often revision; the
problems of cramming, memorizing, and dealing with frustration all
become relevant again.

Physical health and alertness are also important in effective
performance, particularly for performing tasks over a period of

time. Fatigue and poor nutrition are more likely to catch up with
you during the stress of exams than at other times. Thus, you can
undoubtedly get through a two-hour exam Tuesday morning after little sleep Monday night, although you may not be at your best, but
you will have real difficulty studying effectively Tuesday afternoon without catching up on your lost sleep.

Predicting Questions

Predicting exam questions is often advised as an effective
technique for study. The Question step of SQ3R should give you a
good idea of what some of the questions might be. Often instructors
will permit you to look over old examinations for a course. Even
though they change the specific questions each time, the style is
likely to be similar. Also, instructors give you many hints during
the course. Some of these are obvious, such as telling you that a
particular topic usually turns up on the tests. Other hints are
less obvious. Be alert when instructors give an unusually thorough
explanation of some matter—they will probably ask you about it on
the examination.

Attempting to predict examination questions is in keeping
with the principle stated in Chapter 6: the learning situation
should be as similar to the testing situation as possible. You are
not expected merely to write out those questions you anticipate
finding on the test to see how perceptive you are, but rather to
gain practice writing down answers, just as you would in a regular
testing situation.

In predicting multiple-choice items, the main task is deciding
what facts and what broader concepts will be covered by the examination. Since the actual task of writing multiple-choice items is
cumbersome, a more realistic approach to multiple-choice tests is
to jot down only the first part of the question. As an example, go
back to the first paragraph in the section *Preparing for the examination*. You might predict that one question will be "A student
should begin to prepare for his exams . . ." followed by four alternative answers. There is certainly no need to worry about the
four alternatives, but only to know when the preparation should
begin. Knowledge of this point will prepare you for a multiple-
choice question—or a brief essay question or a true-or-false question, for that matter.

Also in the above example, notice that the textbook does not
state specifically when the preparation should begin. Although many
exam questions are drawn directly from the text, others are written
with the assumption that you will make judgments based on what you

have read. In this instance, the correct answer would be something like "as soon as the course begins."

After the first class examination, you can compare your prediction of questions with the actual questions asked. If the professor does not return the examination questions—and objective exams are often not released—he or she may permit you to spend some time in the office studying the question booklet and checking the items against both your answers and your predictions.

At this point, you may also wish to see whether there was a pattern of errors in your performance. Some of the more common reasons that points are lost include: (1) not reading one of the assigned chapters; (2) missing two or three consecutive lectures; (3) reading questions carelessly; (4) using poor or awkward English; (5) wandering away from the main point; (6) writing padded answers or answers that are too sparse; (7) taking inadequate lecture notes for study; (8) and using poor handwriting.

If you can establish a pattern of your shortcomings, not only are you in a better position to predict questions on subsequent tests for that particular faculty member, but you may receive excellent clues to consistent study problems. Predicting questions, of course, should be only an adjunct to study, not the core of study and review.

Group Study

Studying with several other students *can* be a very effective use of time. The word *can* is emphasized because group study is often a waste of time due to engrossing discussions about irrelevant matters or due to inadequate preparation.

When done properly, group sessions have many advantages. First, students are motivated to study before coming to the meeting because they do not like to appear uninformed in front of their friends. Second, group sessions require the students to express themselves aloud to others, a situation that often points up a lack of understanding where they thought they had adequate understanding. Third, having to explain something to others is not only an excellent reinforcement of learning, but utilizes the Recall step of SQ3R in a somewhat different guise; many people have said that they never really understood something until they were forced to explain it to someone else. Fourth, such participation corrects misconceptions and fills in gaps of knowledge. Fifth, hearing what others have to say offers a new slant on the material.

Let us consider some specific suggestions regarding the structure of a group study session. Each group, of course, should make its own adaptations when applying these suggestions. Suppose five students meet together to study American history. Assume that all five have studied previously and have kept reasonably good lecture notes. Just to make the numbers come out easily, assume that the coming examination covers five chapters of reading and 15 class meetings.

Step 1.   Person A begins by looking over his or her lecture notes from the first three class meetings. He or she then asks a question, based on these notes, and selects any other person in the group to answer (the question is stated before the choice of person is made). Person A either agrees with the answer or else calls on someone else to give the correct response. This continues for 15 minutes.

Step 2.   Person B continues the process, drawing from his or her notes from the next three lectures. Persons C, D, and E take their turns leading the group.

Step 3.   After 75 minutes of this, allowing each of the five participants a fair turn, the session is suspended for a 15-minute break.

Step 4.   After the break, someone, perhaps Person A, repeats the same approach, using the textbook material. The group might wish to spend a little more time on the book, since the book usually contains much more content than do the lectures. Of course, if the instructor has said that the exam would be based solely on the book, the group might wish to begin with the textbook and shift to the lecture notes only for a few final minutes.

Many variations of this approach are possible, depending on the nature of the course and the anticipated nature of the coming examination. Some groups add a little incentive by fining members each time they miss a question. The proceeds are used for buying refreshments for the evening.

Group study need not be restricted to the week immediately prior to the examination. Such a group might meet every week or every other week throughout the term. Group study sessions, when properly used, offer the participants an immense advantage both on the subsequent test and in understanding and remembering the course content.

The Final Moments

As the days before the examination dwindle to hours and eventually minutes, students often lose their composure. They realize

that they don't have enough time to complete the necessary review,
and they waste precious time in worthless skimming over their lecture notes and textbook. In the few minutes before the examination,
they attempt to dig in for a final bout of memorizing. It is not
uncommon to see the diehards poring over their books as they walk
into the classroom. The final hour might be used productively, however, but not by flipping pages. This time could be turned to a
final review of memorized terms or a careful reading of the SQ3R
notes, or a review of the lecture-note summaries, or a final attempt to write out in the student's own words the answer to a
particularly complex question that might be asked.

Students who have been able to organize their time now have a
definite edge. They can have a cup of coffee and chat with a friend
for the last hour. A brisk ten-minute walk just prior to the exam
might help clear away the cobwebs left over from long hours of concentration.

DURING THE EXAMINATION

Once you enter the room where the test is to be given, all
time for regrets, self-recriminations, and resolves has passed.
Now the focus is on the task at hand—the examination itself. Hopefully, you enter feeling well prepared, self-confident, relaxed,
and cheerful. But some students worry, become tense, and feel their
hearts banging against their chests, and it certainly does no good
to offer advice regarding past shortcomings at this point. We have,
however, outlined some ideas that might be helpful in taking the
exam.

Procedures for Examinations in General

1. *Read all directions carefully*. On 19 exams out of 20, you
can figure out the directions from reading the first few words, but
occasionally an exam is given with unusual directions.
2. *Look over the entire exam*. Note the number and probable
difficulty of items. Estimate roughly how many items you should be
able to complete in half the allocated time, and gauge your progress accordingly. Check your progress against the remaining time
every once in awhile.
3. *Read each question all the way through*. Many points are
lost on tests by omitting entire parts of essay questions or neg-
lecting to read all the alternatives on objective items. For example:

A.   Discuss the use of the lie detector in contemporary
      police work. Include the pros and cons of its use
      and give examples of success and lack of success.

(It would be very easy to ignore the request for examples in this
question.)

B.   True or False. Mark Twain is the author of *Tom Sawyer*,
      Huckleberry Finn, *Pygmalion*, and *Innocents Abroad*.

(George Bernard Shaw wrote *Pygmalion*, thus making the entire statement false, but if you read this question hurriedly you might not
have picked this up.)

C.   A Registered Nurse is:
      1.   certified by the State Medical Licensing Board
      2.   capable of performing operations
      3.   always kind and thoughtful
      4.   licensed by the State Board of Examiners in Nursing

(If you had not read the final alternative, you might have accepted
alternative 1, which comes close to being correct.)

4.   *Understand the scoring system*. In an essay exam, each
question might count the same number of points or they might vary
in value. In the latter case, you may wish to direct more time and
energy to the questions worth the most points. In most essay exams,
the lowest score you can obtain on any particular question is zero;
thus a bad guess is worth no less than leaving the space blank.
However, you may know a little more than you realize, so attempt to
discern the general meaning of the question and write down something
that seems to fit. The reward is frequently partial credit—if you
show you know at least a little about the topic.

In most instances, you should answer every item on an objective test. Sometimes, however, the instructor uses a correction-
for-chance factor, often termed a penalty for guessing. The theory
is that a second-grader could randomly fill in the lines of the answer sheet, and, assuming a multiple-choice test with four alternatives, this second-grader would obtain a score of 25% correct, just
by chance. The correction-for-chance factor sets up a formula that
would cause this second-grader to get a score of zero. The formula
is

$$S = R - \frac{W}{A - 1} \, .$$

S is score; *R* is number correct; *W* is number wrong; *A* is number of
alternative answers. You may wish to check this formula out with
the hypothetical second-grader above or on a true/false test. This
type of scoring is cumbersome and, except for nationally standardized examinations, rarely used. However, even if it is, the odds
are with you by answering every item anyway, assuming you can
eliminate at least one alternative as being incorrect.

5. *Do not spend too much time on any one item*. If an item
puzzles you, go on to the next, but be certain to make some sort
of mark to remind you of the omission. It is usually not a good
idea to spend a disproportionately long time on any one item until
you have completed the entire exam. Not only does this assure you
of having time to answer as many correctly as possible, but a later
question sometimes helps you recall the answer to an earlier one.

6. *Go over the exam carefully when you have finished*. This
is your opportunity to pick up errors and omissions on essay exams
and mistakes on objective exams. An excellent way to check your
objective test answers, if time is available, is to look back at
each question and give the answer you feel is most appropriate,
without looking at your original answer. Then check your later answers against your initial responses.

The value of reading over essay questions is similar to proofreading a paper or lab report: you are likely to spot misspellings,
factual errors, and errors in grammar and punctuation. You also
might be able to add relevant information and ideas that had not
occurred to you earlier.

Procedures for Objective Examinations

1. *Avoid careless errors* when using IBM answer sheets. You
are usually advised to mark heavily between the indicated lines
and to avoid making stray marks on your paper, since they might be
counted as errors by the machine. Also, an A student can end up
with an F grade merely by marking answers by the wrong numbers, a
simple error to make with electronically scored answer sheets.
This mistake usually occurs when the student omits an item, meaning to come back to it, and then goes on to mark each subsequent
answer one space above the proper number.

2. *Be careful with words* such as *all, never, always, tendency, probably*. The first three terms often (but not *always*) turn
basically correct statements into incorrect statements, while the
last two terms require a careful evaluation of the statement's
meaning. For example:

"All college graduates have above-average intelligence."
(False) "College graduates tend to have above-average intelligence." (True)

3. *Do not hesitate to change alternatives* if you feel reasonably certain that your later judgment is correct.

Procedures for Essay Examinations

1. For long essay questions, *a brief outline of the response
is useful*. This may be 20 to 30 words, consisting of words and
brief phrases that express the essence of the discussion. For example:

Question

Discuss the contribution that a course in improved study
skills might make to a lower-echelon business executive.

Answer outline

—probably a young woman or man; could have a good future
—must prepare to read many reports quickly, remember
  information well
—can learn to listen
—efficient utilization of time for work and play
—improved office conditions for concentration
—principles of motivation, memory, learning

2. *Longer essay questions require more concern for organization* than do those taking only five or six minutes to write.
A brief introduction and a good concluding statement are important.
The introductory statement might either present an overview or just
serve as a lead-in. The concluding statement should pull the entire
answer together, perhaps indicating a future direction or course of
action, evaluating what has been said, or providing a summary
statement. Also, organization might call for presenting material in
a proper time sequence, explaining or defending statements that are
not obviously true, and developing important lines of thought beyond the bare statement of fact.

Question

Discuss the community college as a phenomenon in higher
education today.

Answer

Following the Second World War, attendance in community
colleges increased rapidly, leading to the establishment
of many new schools. . . . It seems obvious, for the reasons stated above, that the role of the community college
will continue to increase in importance, especially if
the present demand by older and retired persons for continuing education does not diminish.

3. *The use of good grammar, spelling, punctuation, and handwriting is highly desirable.* Faculty members, of course, vary
greatly in the degree of importance they place on these skills.
4. *A good long answer is better, most of the time, than a
good short answer, and a mediocre long answer is better than a
mediocre short answer, but a good short answer is better than a
mediocre long answer.*
5. *When given the option of several questions, choose the
easiest first, but be certain to judge the time correctly* so that
you can answer as many as are required. Do not spend half your
period answering one question because you know so much about the
topic, leaving only the remaining half to answer the three remaining questions.
6. *Leave some space at the end of every question*, if you can,
in the event you wish to return later to add some more material.
7. *Be certain to answer the question that was asked*, not another question. This means reading the question carefully and not
wandering from the original purpose as you write. There are several
terms used in essay exams that students frequently pay little attention to. If you are asked to *list* or *outline*, do not give a
lengthy *description*; a question calling for an *evaluation* should
not be answered by either a *discussion* or a piece of propaganda;
when asked to *summarize*, do not give an *example*. Other terms frequently seen include *compare, contrast, identify, illustrate, explain, integrate, relate, define,* and *present the pros and cons.*
Although there are obvious overlaps among some of these terms, each
should suggest a slightly different approach to the question.

The stress associated with college exams probably cannot be
totally eliminated; perhaps some stress is even helpful in moti-
vating you to accomplish more. However, there are ways of reducing
stress and text anxiety and of improving performance, not merely
because grades are based on exam scores but because studying for
and taking course exams can be a useful learning opportunity in
itself.

Examples of Good and Poor Answers to Essay Questions

1. Evaluate the motion picture as an art form.

> The motion picture is an amazingly important technological advancement in art and entertainment. Rising to importance in an area of Los Angeles known as Hollywood, movies are important economically to all the country and have become important abroad as well. They enable people of one country to obtain a good picture of what living in another country is like. I think the motion picture is a real art form.

Student A

> The motion picture certainly has the potential to be an art form, but commercial needs have placed the emphasis upon entertainment value rather than art. However, in some films, both U.S. and foreign, real artistry is shown in the use of color, movement, angle shots, and so forth. Also, young people all around the world are producing exciting experimental films on very low budgets that may eventually point the way to the full realization of cinema as art.

Student B

Comments: Although the second student expressed herself much better than the first, the most important difference between the two was in their ability to evaluate. Student A made a few appropriate statements about the importance of movies, but they did not have direct relevance to movies as an art form. At the end of his comments, he states that "the motion picture is a real art form," but this statement is certainly inadequate under the circumstances.

2. List the four Presidents preceding Eisenhower, and state one accomplishment of each.

Truman - war in Korea
Roosevelt - depression, war in Europe
Hoover - helped Belgians
Coolidge - prosperity

Student C

Calvin Coolidge - president during times of great prosperity
Herbert Hoover - developed programs to offset the depression
F. D. Roosevelt - led the country through the depression
and through the Second World War
Harry Truman - prosecuted the Korean War almost to its
conclusion

Student D

Comments: Student C gives a minimally adequate response that
would probably receive only partial credit. War and depression are
certainly not accomplishments, and Hoover's work with the Belgians,
although well known, took place long before his presidency. Student
C presents the kernel of the answer, but no more. Student D also
answered briefly and without full sentences, but he stated enough
to indicate that he had fuller knowledge than Student C.

3.   What is SQ3R and how does it work?

SQ3R is a method for reading textbooks with greater
efficiency. It works by making the student pay
greater attention to what he reads. This is achieved
through five steps: (1) Survey - skim the chapter
and read the summary; (2) Question - turn
headings into questions, (3) Read - read the section
under the heading, (4) Recall - answer the
question of the Q step; (5) Review - review the
notes and perhaps skim again and read summary.

Student E

SQ3R is when you read textbooks
by using five things -- you survey, question,
read, recall, review. You survey when
you look over the chapter; you question
when you make up questions; you
read when you read; you recall
when you answer questions; then
you review.

Student F

Comments: The first answer is brief and fairly good; it covers both parts of the question. The second answer contains several errors: it never states what SQ3R is; it uses very poor grammar and rhetoric; it answers superficially; it offers some redundancies; and it is vague.

4.   Compare white-collar work with blue-collar work.

> White collar workers have clean jobs and blue collar workers have dirty jobs, so they wear blue collars that don't show the dirt too much.

Student G

> Types of jobs are classified by the color of the worker's collar because men wear white shirts for office work and blue shirts for skilled trades, manual work, and other semi-skilled and unskilled jobs; their work is clean and has higher prestige than blue collar work, although not always higher pay. Blue collar workers may get dirty on some of their jobs, and they range in skills from a totally unskilled person to a highly skilled plumber or electrician. White collar workers include office boys and company presidents.

Student H

The sort of work a person does helps him decide whether he wants to wear a white collar or a blue collar. White collar workers have cleaner jobs and earn more money, while blue collar workers are dirty and poorer. This is because people don't like to take dirty jobs because dirt in our culture has always been thought of as low class. Low class people get dirtier than higher class people, because they do not understand so much about good health and keeping clean, and they even sometimes do not have the money to do so.

Student I

Comments: Student G gives a very brief answer and makes one valid point; however, she misses the real significance of the question. Student H's response is a bit repetitive, but he does what the question asks and covers the ground fairly well, giving some relevant information not directly asked for. Student I begins with some interesting ideas, but becomes sidetracked and loses sight of the original question.

SUMMARY OF IMPORTANT IDEAS

1. Examinations are a major cause of anger, anxiety, fear, and complaints.
2. Attitudes toward the particular examination or toward examinations in general can affect performance.
3. There are several types of examinations: open-book and closed-book, take-home and in-class, nationally standarized and local, verbal and performance, and essay and objective.
4. Preparing for exams must be a continuing process.
5. One of the best ways to prepare for exams is to predict questions and then practice answering the questions you predicted.
6. Studying with others can be very helpful, but only when the group does not lapse into general discussions.
7. A number of techniques for taking exams can improve performance. Among these are (1) reading all directions carefully, (2) looking over the entire exam before beginning, (3) reading each question all the way through, (4) understanding the scoring system, and (5) not spending too much time on any one item.
8. Specific techniques applied to essay exams or to objective exams are also helpful.

EXERCISES

1. Write ten questions that might be used for this course: five essay items, two true/false items, two multiple-choice items, and one matching question.

2. Select any course you wish (other than this one) and predict questions for the next examination. If an essay test is used, predict between 10 and 15 questions, even if the exam itself will not have this many. If an objective exam is used, predict 25 to 30 questions by writing down the theme of each question, not the entire item.

After the examination, check to see how many questions you predicted. If necessary, ask the instructor for permission to look over the examination in his or her office. Indicate the proportion of questions taken from lectures, the textbook, outside reading, and other sources.

3. Write questions for this course using each of the following terms. Answer the questions briefly.

Outline: _____

_____

_____

_____

Evaluate: _____

_____

_____

_____

Contrast: _____

_____

_____

_____

Differentiate: _____

_____

_____

_____

Justify: _____

_____

_____

_____

Illustrate: _____

_____

_____

_____

Select two more terms:

a. _____

_____

_____

_____

b. _____

_____

_____

_____

Taking Examinations

   Try to recall your preparations for the last examination you took. Check those procedures you followed. Comment on the procedures you followed. Comment on the procedures you did not follow—what was the effect of not following them? After you take the next exam in the same course, fill out this form again.

	Last exam		Next exam	
	Check ▼	Or comment ▼	Check ▼	Or comment ▼
1. I read all directions carefully.				
2. I looked over the entire exam first.				
3. I read every question all the way through.				
4. I understood the scoring system				
5. I did not spend too much time on one item.				
6. I went over the exam carefully after finishing.				

	Last exam		Next exam	
	Check ▼	Or comment ▼	Check ▼	Or comment ▼
7. I outlined long essay questions.				
8. I attempted to use good grammar.				
9. I attempted to use good handwriting.				
10. I was careful to understand what the question asked for.				
11. I estimated time correctly.				
12. I looked the exam over carefully when returned.				

OBJECTIVES

1. To encourage proper use of library facilities.

2. To describe, with examples, the use of the card catalogue.

3. To present the various classifying systems.

4. To discuss, in detail, many major reference books and related materials.

Chapter 9

Using
the Library

The past two decades have seen what is often termed "the information explosion." The number of publications has increased so tremendously that scientists have developed information-retrieval systems permitting computers to be programmed to ferret out all the articles and books on a given topic. At present many libraries offer, usually for a fee, literature-search services that produce a computer printout listing references on a particular topic. Eventually you may be able to hand the librarian a code number denoting a topic and a few moments later receive a list of publications on the subject, with each reference accompanied by a brief paragraph summarizing its contents. Until that day arrives, however, you must know how to use the available library facilities as they are organized at the present time. If you are skilled in doing this, you will be able to locate library materials quickly and easily, and you will end up with the books, periodical articles, and other materials you need. If you lack these skills, you may spend a lot of time searching for the desired information or you may completely miss some of the materials most important to your course work.

Library collections today often include nonbook materials: a great variety of films, slides, and audio and video recordings, together with the equipment for using them, plus teaching machines, computer services, and much more. Materials in these nonbook media may be listed in the card catalog along with the printed books or

*This chapter was written by George M. Rolling, Social Sciences Librarian, John F. Kennedy Library, California State University, Los Angeles. I also thank Carolyn Crawford and Clayton Brown for their participation.

they may be indexed separately. Likewise they may be shelved with
the books or elsewhere. Although we will use the term "library"
throughout this chapter, it may be called something else on your
campus. When the newer media materials are housed with the more
traditional library materials, the whole complex may be called a
"learning resources center" or a "media center." This trend is
particularly strong in community colleges. In any event, keep in
mind that these nonbook materials will probably also be available
to you.

EXPLORING THE LIBRARY

There are occasions, usually before examination and term-paper
pressures mount, when nothing is more pleasant than wandering up
and down the long aisles of stacks browsing through the books. For
the most part, however, students wish to locate materials as rapidly as possible. To do this, they must know their way around the
library, and they must know the library's rules and procedures.

To help you use the library, some libraries prepare a special
handbook for distribution to students. A library floor plan is
frequently part of the handbook or may be available separately. If
no plan is available, sketch one for yourself, listing in detail
the location of articles for which you have use and add other areas
as they become relevant to your work. A floor plan should include
the location of those sections containing subject matter that is
related to your courses and to your personal interests and hobbies.
In diagramming a reference room, it's a good idea to include the
specific locations of some of the more commonly used reference
books.

Also during this exploration, find out how to complete the
forms for checking out materials. Knowing in advance how to fill
out a form correctly saves valuable time when you need something
quickly. The length of time you may keep a book varies with the
book. For example, although normal loan periods may be two weeks or
longer, limited-loan books are usually due in two or three days or
a week, reserve books are usually lent for anywhere from one hour
to two days, and special-collection and reference books usually may
not be removed at all. In some libraries, older periodicals and
rarely used books have been relegated to storage stacks.

Purchasing a copy of a library manual may be advisable, particularly if the library is very large and lacks an adequate, up-
to-date handbook. A library manual provides a detailed list of directions for using a library and includes information about the
kinds of reference books and nonbook materials available. Some of
the more widely recommended manuals include:

1. Aldrich, Ella V. *Using books and libraries* (5th ed.). Englewood Cliffs, N.J.: Prentice-Hall, 1967.
2. Cook, Margaret Gerry. *The new library key* (3rd ed.). New York: H. W. Wilson, 1975.
3. Gates, Jean Kerr. *Guide to the use of books and libraries* (3rd ed.). New York: McGraw-Hill, 1974.
4. Lolley, John. *Your library: What's in it for you*. New York: Wiley, 1974.

CLASSIFYING AND CATALOGING

The most direct way to locate library materials is to use the card catalog. Along with books and periodicals, nonbook materials may be listed there (in which case they will be designated as such by part of the call number), or they may be in separate indexes. Ask a librarian to explain the system used in your college's library. The following listing shows the diversity of nonbook materials: audiocassettes, audiorecords, audiotapes, cards, charts, filmloops, filmstrips, games, kits, microcards, microfiche, microfilm, microprint, puppets, realia, videocassettes, videorecords, and videotapes.

The following explanation uses the term "book," although nonbook materials, if they are entered in the main card catalog rather than in a separate index, will probably be entered in the same way.

In most libraries, every book is cataloged at least three times: by subject, by author's name (last name first, of course), and by title. Generally, but not always, a book that is part of a series is also entered in the catalog under the name of that series, unless the series name begins with the name of a commercial publisher (for example "The McGraw-Hill series in . . . "). Subject-card headings are usually printed at the top of the card, either in red or in capital letters.

Author cards and title cards provide the same information but permit you to find the location of a book more rapidly, assuming you know either the last name of the author or the title of the book. Most libraries used to file all their catalog cards in one alphabetical arrangement (called "the dictionary catalog"), but the tendency in recent years has been to place the subject cards in a separate file from the author, title, and series cards. (This system is called "the divided catalog.")

Cross-reference cards, which refer you to other topics and subject cards, are also useful. When the word "see" is used, the materials desired are listed not under the original word but under the word referred to. The words "see also" mean that the present heading contains some references and that additional materials will

```
                    UNITED STATES--POLITICS AND
                    GOVERNMENT--1977

   E                Shogan, Robert.
   872                 Promises to keep : Carter's first
   S53              hundred days / Robert Shogan. -- New
   1977             York : Crowell, c1977.
                       x, 300 p., [4] leaves of plates :
                    ill.; 24 cm.

                       Includes bibliographical references
                    and index.
                       ISBN 0-690-01497-X

                       1.  Carter, Jimmy, 1924-
                    2. Presidents--United States--Election
                    --1976.  3. United States--Politics and
                    government--1977- I. Title.

   SU        771204                  CLS
   2593332                           77-22818
                                     BJ 5509785
   E872.S53 1977
```

Subject card

```
   E                Shogan, Robert.
   872                 Promises to keep : Carter's first
   S53              hundred days / Robert Shogan. -- New
   1977             York : Crowell, c1977.
                       x, 300 p., [4] leaves of plates :
                    ill.; 24 cm.

                       Includes bibliographical references
                    and index.
                       ISBN 0-690-01497-X

                       1. Carter, Jimmy, 1924-
                    2. Presidents--United States--Election
                    --1976.  3. United States--Politics and
                    government--1977- I. Title.

   AT        771204                  CLS
   2593332                           77-22818
                                     BJ 5509785
   E872.S53 1977
```

Author card

```
              Promises to keep.

E             Shogan, Robert.
872               Promises to keep : Carter's first
S53           hundred days / Robert Shogan. -- New
1977          York : Crowell, c1977.
                  x, 300 p., [4] leaves of plates :
              ill.; 24 cm.

                  Includes bibliographical references
              and index.
                  ISBN 0-690-01497-X

                  1. Carter, Jimmy, 1924-
              2. Presidents--United States--Election
              --1976.  3. United States--Politics and
              government--1977- I. Title.
AT            771204           CLS
2593332                       77-22818
                              BJ 5509785
E872.S53 1977
```

Title card

```
              U. S. - Presidents

                  see

              Presidents - United States
```

Cross-reference card

be found under the indicated term. Many libraries don't file "see
also" cards but instead refer you to a book that lists subject headings.

Initially, you may find the filing arrangement in the card
catalog confusing. Although you can usually find the desired card by
looking up the title, the author, or the subject, alphabetically,
there are some rules worth remembering:

1. The articles "a," "an," and "the" are not used when
    determining the alphabetical placement of a card.
    Thus, *The Normal Personality* will be filed under
    "Normal," not "The."
2. Historical material may be filed chronologically
    rather than in normal alphabetical order. For example,
    "United States—History—Colonial period" may precede
    "United States—History—Civil War."
3. Subject cards that contain an inverted element may be
    filed after cards without such an element. For exam-
    ple, "Psychology—Methodology" may precede "Psy-
    chology, Industrial."
4. In catalogs where subject entry cards are included
    with other cards, books by an author will precede
    books about that author.
5. If the same word is used for a person, a place, and
    a title, the cards are filed in that order.
6. Parts of books are sometimes cataloged, particularly
    when different authors have contributed different
    sections.
7. Some libraries include periodical titles in the gen-
    eral card catalog; some have a separate periodical
    file; and some include periodicals in both places.
8. Abbreviations are filed as though they were spelled
    out. Thus, "Dr." is filed as "Doctor" and "St. Louis:
    is filed as "Saint Louis." But ask your librarian
    about the filing of "Mrs." and "Ms."
9. Numerals are also filed as though they were spelled
    out. If the first word in the title is "50," look
    under "fifty."
10. Different libraries follow slightly different pro-
    cedures in filing catalog cards. Inquire at the desk
    if you can't find a card for materials that you think
    should be in the library.

Once you locate the card, make an accurate note of the code numbers
or letters in the upper left-hand corner. This designation is the
book's "call number," and it indicates where in the library the

book is to be found. Books are grouped by subject matter, and several classification schemes are in use. Most libraries use either the Library of Congress system (see Table 10-1) or the Dewey decimal system (see Table 10-2).

Table 10-1. Library of Congress Classification System

Classification	Subject
A	General works, general encyclopedias, museums, societies
B-BJ	Philosophy, psychology
BL-BX	Religion
C	Auxiliary sciences of history, including archaeology, archives, numismatics, genealogy, and general biography
D	History (general and Old World)
E-F	History of America, including geography of individual countries
G	Geography, anthropology, folklore, dance, sports, recreation and games
H-HA	General social sciences, statistics
HB-HJ	Economics
HM-HX	Sociology
J-JX	Political science
K	Law
L-LT	Education
M-MT	Music
N-NX	Fine arts
P-PT	Language and literature
Q-QC	General science, mathematics, astronomy, physics
QD-QK	Chemistry, geology, natural history, botany
QL-QR	Zoology, human anatomy, physiology, bacteriology
R-RZ	Medicine
S-SK	Agriculture, plants, animal industry
T-TX	Technology, engineering, photography, home economics
U-UH	Military science
V-VM	Naval science
Z	Bibliography, library science

Table 10-2. Dewey Decimal Classification System

Classification	Subject
000-099	General works, journalism, library science
100-199	Philosophy, psychology
200-299	Religion
300-369	Sociology, statistics, political science, economics, law
370-379	Education
380-399	Trade, communications, customs, folklore
400-499	Languages
500-509	General science
510-519	Mathematics
520-549	Astronomy, physics, chemistry, crystallography, mineralogy
550-599	Earth sciences, paleontology, anthropology, biology, botany, zoology
600-639	Medicine, nursing, pharmacy, engineering, agriculture
640-649	Home economics
650-659	Business
660-699	Chemical technology, metallurgy, manufacturing, building
700-769	Art, architecture, sculpture, interior decoration, painting, prints
770-779	Photography
780-789	Music
790-799	Recreation
800-899	Literature
900-999	History, geography, travel

Some books won't be found on the shelves under their classification numbers. These exceptions include books that are too large to fit on the normal library shelves, books that receive a great deal of of use and therefore may be in a limited-loan or reserve room, books that are considered very valuable or fragile, and reference books. The abbreviation "ref" or "R" above the call number indicates that the book is a reference book and cannot circulate; some of these books are in the library's reference room. Oversize books, limited-loan or reserve books, and books kept by the librarian are identified by notes or symbols on the catalog card. Nonbook materials are also identified as such on the catalog card.

Some college libraries have closed stacks, and you must write down the call number, along with other identifying data, of the book

you want and have someone working in the library bring the book to
you. Open-stack libraries permit you to find your own books. When
you can't find a particular book in an open-stack library, it may be
in circulation, misshelved elsewhere in the library, or waiting to
be reshelved. If it isn't in the immediate vicinity, an attendant at
the loan desk may be able to determine where it is and when it is
due to be returned.

PERIODICAL INDEXES

You have probably become accustomed to using a variety of
magazines as sources for term papers and other research, but most
likely you haven't used professional journals in your research as
yet. However, there are hundreds of professional journals, containing many thousands of articles—often but not always highly technical—that serve as authoritative sources for up-to-date information.
Finding the appropriate articles in the appropriate journals can be
a problem, not only for undergraduates but also for more sophisticated researchers. As a result, many indexes are available to help
you locate relevant materials rapidly. In addition to listing references, some indexes also provide brief abstracts of the periodical
articles and other library materials—such as books and government
documents—that they index. Here is a list of representative indexes:

Education

Child Development Abstracts
Current Index to Journals in Education
Education Index
Exceptional Child Education Abstracts
State Education Journal Index
Subject Index to Children's Magazines

Science and technology

Applied Science and Technology Index
Biological Abstracts
Biological and Agricultural Index
Chemical Abstracts
Cumulative Index to Nursing Literature
Engineering Index
Index Medicus
Mathematical Reviews
Science Abstracts
Zoological Record

Humanities

Abstracts of English Studies
Art Index
Biography Index
Book Review Digest
Book Review Index
British Humanities Index
Current Book Review Citations
Essay and General Literature Index
Humanities Index
Index to Book Reviews in the Humanities
Music Index

Social sciences and business

Accountants' Index
America: History and Life
Business Education Index
Historical Abstracts
Index to Legal Periodicals
Psychological Abstracts
Public Affairs Information Service (PAIS) Bulletin
Social Sciences Index
Sociological Abstracts

In addition to specialized indexes and abstracts, several general listings are available. The well-known *Readers' Guide to Periodical Literature*, although not covering the more technical and academic articles, can still be of considerable use, as can the *Nineteenth Century Readers' Guide*. Also, the *Catholic Periodical and Literature Index* is a useful index and is broad enough in scope to be of general interest. For those interested in news events, the *New York Times Index* provides a detailed alphabetical index of subjects and names from 1913 to the present. Other newspapers that are now indexed include the *Wall Street Journal, Christian Science Monitor, Chicago Tribune, Los Angeles Times, New Orleans Times-Picayune,* and *Washington Post*.

The first step in using these periodical indexes is to determine the subject heading under which the required material is likely to appear. (In general, these publications are more helpful when you want to compile a list of articles and books that deal with a particular subject rather than a list of articles and books written by a particular author.) Because not everyone thinks of subjects in the same way, you may need imagination and flexibility to find the proper heading. Don't hesitate to ask a librarian for assistance.

After you have located the proper heading, the next step is to decide which periodicals will best cover the topic. You might look through a couple, or you might seek the suggestions of the librarian immediately. Eventually you will learn what each index offers.

The third step is to learn the most efficient way to locate the desired references in particular indexes. Many periodical indexes are organized by some logical sequence of topics and have indexes of their own in the back, in which the topics are arranged alphabetically and you are referred to the proper page or proper item. In other instances, the entire volume is arranged alphabetically by topic—for example, the *Readers' Guide to Periodical Literature*.

Once you locate an article in the index, write down the bibliographic citation completely and accurately. You will need the complete citation when giving references for a term paper, and you'll save yourself a return trip to the index.

Other Reference Sources

Periodical indexes, of course, are not the only reference source in the library; numerous other sources exist. For example, almost everyone has used a general encyclopedia; it was probably the most widely used reference in high school. However, the college library offers several special-subject encyclopedias, such as the *Encyclopedia of Education, International Encyclopedia of the Social Sciences, Encyclopedia of Philosophy, McGraw-Hill Encyclopedia of Science and Technology, Encyclopedia of Religion and Ethics,* and *Encyclopedia of World Art*.

In similar fashion, most students are familiar with the usefulness of a good dictionary, but many are unaware that numerous special dictionaries exist: *The Mathematics Dictionary, A Comprehensive Dictionary of Psychological and Psychoanalytical Terms, Dictionary of the Social Sciences, Webster's Geographical Dictionary, International Cyclopedia of Music and Musicians, Dictionary of Education,* and others.

In addition to encyclopedias and dictionaries, the college library contains handbooks, pamphlets, manuals, annuals or yearbooks, statistical abstracts, almanacs, atlases, biographical dictionaries, and so forth. Here is a list of other reference books, many of which are not familiar to college students.

Printed catalogs

British Museum. *General Catalogue of Printed Books*. Holdings of the major British research library through 1955 with supplements for later years.

United States. Library of Congress. *Catalog of Printed Cards*. A comprehensive listing of the holdings of the Library of Congress, containing author entries only, with supplements for the years after 1942. The *National Union Catalog* is a continuation of this listing, begun in 1956, and includes some titles held by other American and Canadian libraries. A *National Union Catalog, Pre-1956 Imprints* is in process of publication.

United States. Library of Congress. *Catalog. Books: Subjects*. This complements the *National Union Catalog* and is continued by the *Subject Catalog* of the Library of Congress.

Trade bibliographies

Cumulative Book Index (CBI). World list of books in the English language, published each month except August, and cumulative. An author/title/subject listing. Complete bibliography exclusive of government documents, maps, sheet music, inexpensive and paperbound editions, pamphlets, tracts, propaganda, and other issues of local or temporary nature.

Biblio. A catalog of works published in the French language worldwide. Published monthly from 1934 until its merger with *Bibliographie de la France* in 1972 to form *Bibliographie de la France—Biblio*. Annual cumulation of listings published as *Les livres de l'année—Biblio*, beginning in 1971.

Publishers' Trade List Annual. A listing of books in print by publisher.

Books in Print. An annual author/title index to *Publishers' Trade List Annual*.

Subject Guide to Books in Print. A companion volume to *Books in Print*.

Paperbound Books in Print. A semiannual author/title/subject listing.

Libros en Venta en Hispanoamérica y España. Books in print in Spanish, serving twenty countries of the Americas and Spain. Author/title/subject listing, published in 1974.

Bibliographies and periodical directories of a general
nature

Bibliographic Index. A cumulative bibliography of bibliographies from 1000 to 1900 periodicals, also of bibliographies
published separately or in books. Both foreign and domestic
coverage. Published annually.

Besterman World Bibliographies. New editions, published in
the 1970s, of the work previously published under one title,
A World Bibliography of Bibliographies. Also includes bibliographic catalogs, calendars, abstracts, digests, indexes,
and the like.

Dissertation Abstracts International. A compilation of abstracts of doctoral dissertations submitted to University
Microfilms, Inc., by cooperating universities. Now appears
in two separately bound sections monthly: A. Humanities
and social sciences and B. Sciences and engineering.

Index Translationum. International bibliography of transla-
tions, published annually by UNESCO. Includes literary,
scientific, educational, and cultural works published in
pamphlet or book form and cross-indexed under authors,
translators, and publishers.

Ulrich's International Periodicals Directory. Published
every two years. Titles are grouped in subject classifica-
tions arranged alphabetically. Indicates the indexing and
abstracting services available for each title. Includes list
of periodicals that have ceased publication since the previous edition of the directory. Does not include annuals,
monographs, and series publications, or most government
documents.

USING THE LIBRARY

Before the freshman year ends, students are frequently required to write at least one term paper. The library can be used
most effectively if you first ask yourself five questions:

1. Is this a subject only of current importance, will
   the information be contained in older writings, or will
   I need to investigate both newer and older materials?
2. Is an encyclopedia a good place to begin, so that I
   can obtain a general overview?

3. If the topic is current, what is the most appropriate
    periodical index to use?
4. Can the library provide any additional resources, be-
    yond books and periodical articles, that might be valu-
    able—for example, government documents, pamphlets,
    materials reproduced in microform (such as microfiche
    and microfilm), map collections, historical collections,
    audio and video recordings, graduate theses, art col-
    lections, or special-subject collections?
5. Will library resources be the only sources for this
    paper, or should I use other approaches, such as inter-
    viewing, collection of original data, or writing to
    specialists?

Although your personal exploration is valuable, a librarian
usually can be of considerable help in answering the preceding
questions. Although librarians are accustomed to tackling even the
vaguest of inquiries, the more specific the question, the better the
answer.

Often you will find yourself referred to the Reserve or
Limited-Loan Room, which contains those materials that have such extensive use that they need special attention. Instructors normally
inform the library of those books they want "on reserve" or "on
limited loan." They will often do this when the library has only one
or two copies of a book or article that is assigned to 40 to 50
students to read. The length of time a book may be borrowed is limited, thus permitting its wider circulation. Also, the fines for returning the book late are much larger than usual.

Libraries frequently offer services other than the use of
books and periodicals. For example, some libraries have a microform
collection and facilities for its use. Microform is often used when
materials are either too bulky to store, too expensive to purchase,
or too difficult to obtain in the original. A second example of the
wide range of services is the opportunity to borrow or rent phono-
graph records, audio cassettes, or artwork for personal enjoyment;
some colleges even have record and cassette players available. A
paperback collection is often provided to permit students to sit and
read what they please at their leisure. And interlibrary-loan arrangements often allow students to borrow hard-to-get books from
other libraries and to obtain photocopies of periodical articles
held by other libraries.

Books and other library materials are the lifeblood of a college, providing intellectual nourishment to faculty members and students alike. Circulating and otherwise making available the college's lifeblood is the task of the heart of the college—the
library.

SUMMARY OF IMPORTANT IDEAS

1. Some libraries provide a special handbook for students.
2. The most direct way to locate materials is through the card
    catalog. Nonbook materials may be listed in the card catalog
    or in special indexes.
3. The card catalog contains a variety of information, including
    the author's name and year of birth (if known), the publish-
    ing company, and the number by which the item is classified.
4. The major schemes for classifying books by subject are the
    Library of Congress system and the Dewey decimal system.
5. A large number of indexes and abstracts are available to
    enable a more rapid location of periodical articles and other
    materials.
6. Although personal exploration on the part of the student is
    very valuable, the librarian is of considerable help in find-
    ing materials.
7. Libraries frequently offer services such as circulating art,
    phonorecord, and audio-cassette collections, photoduplication,
    microform collections and facilities for use, government docu-
    ments, maps, and interlibrary-loan service.

OBJECTIVES

1. To emphasize the importance of term papers and other written materials.

2. To outline the steps in preparing a term paper.

3. To provide specific examples of notes for term papers, outlines for term papers, and other aspects of these papers.

Chapter 10

Written Communications

Ours is a verbal society. Although manual dexterity, physical strength, motor coordination, and speed all have their place, it is words that are crucial in producing the goods and services our society requires. Advertising copywriters, secretaries, and high school English teachers obviously need verbal skills but sales managers, nurses, policemen, accountants, and engineers have just as great a need for verbal skill.

One of the most common complaints that employers direct at schools today is that students do not sufficiently develop the ability to communicate in writing. Business people who cannot write good letters, police officers who cannot write accurate accident reports, and nurses who cannot write clear statements of their observations are all at a distinct disadvantage in performing their jobs effectively.

A written message may be more difficult to transmit accurately than an oral message because of the lack of immediate feedback. When you speak with a person or give an oral report, you can observe their reaction to your words. With a written presentation, whether it be an informal letter or a lengthy term paper, you have to wait until later for the audience reaction. And by then it is too late to make changes.

Written presentations differ from oral communications in three other ways: (1) Written messages cannot make use of tone of voice, pauses, gestures, or facial expressions to communicate meaning. (2) The written form of English is more conservative than the spoken form. It is usually speech that initiates the new and writing that holds on to the old. (3) Writing is a more self-conscious, deliberate activity than speaking. In a sense, speaking is natural and writing is artificial.

Any given written communication may have one or more purposes.
It may attempt to integrate the ideas of others, to express opinions and conclusions, to propose new ideas, to report observations,
to persuade others, to entertain or amuse, to enlighten, to elicit
a particular emotional response, and so forth. In college, you may
be assigned a written report involving any or all of these goals.
Themes in English class are likely to run the gamut from cautious
and accurate reporting to propagandistic and emotional exhortation.
In other classes, a report or term paper most commonly calls for
accurate reporting, integrating the ideas of others, and expressing
your own thinking and conclusions, usually based on careful analysis and research.

I'm not going to attempt any discussion of grammar here, but
I would encourage you to obtain a copy of a good handbook of the
English language and to make the most of the brief opportunity you
will have to study grammar in your freshman English courses (even
though it may not seem brief at the time).

THE SIGNIFICANCE OF TERM PAPERS

Term papers have several purposes. First, they give you the
opportunity to pursue a particular topic in greater depth than the
classroom situation allows. Every course should have at least a
few topics that motivate you to investigate further, and the term
paper allows for this. Simultaneously, you develop a little bit
of expert knowledge. You can know more about something than most
of the other students and, on occasion, more than the instructor.
This knowledge might be related to vocational goals, to your personal interests, or to leisure activities.

Second, working on a topic for a term paper acquaints you
with the wide variety of source materials and how to find them.
You become sensitive to the differences between primary source
material and secondary source material (what would you assume this
difference to be?). You learn about the people who are particularly
noted for their contributions to this topic. You become familiar
with the college library and the amazing variety of information
sources in the library (see Chapter 9). Each time you write a term
paper, you broaden your knowledge in these ways.

Third, a term paper offers the experience of working independently. When a term paper is assigned, you will need to plan
your time, to locate sources of information, and to evaluate con-
flicting statements. In later courses, when your work requires a
more in-depth study, your work on term papers will have given you
some relevant experience.

Fourth, term papers often call for bringing together and evaluating the work of several individuals. You may also be expected to come up with new ideas of your own.

Because of the opportunity to explore an area in depth and because of the independence you are permitted, you may well recall term papers as your most valuable experience in a course. Even in courses you don't care for, writing a term paper may become a stimulating experience.

WORKING ON THE PAPER

Professors vary in their expectations for term papers. Some want scholarly reports; others prefer creative and innovative thinking; still others are mainly concerned with finding evidence of your having read widely in the selected area. Usually the way a term paper is assigned offers substantial clues as to the type of paper preferred. In most instances, wide reading and creative thinking are pertinent to the job. Instructor preferences for style also vary. Some desire a well-ordered, highly structured approach, while others enjoy informality or literary flavor.

A well-written term paper (1) has something to say, (2) supports what it has to say with good research and intelligent thought, and (3) says it in a literate way and with proper use of the mechanics of language. Although individual cases vary, I have outlined below a basic plan of action for writing a major term paper. The plan may be modified as necessary for briefer papers, for specialized papers and laboratory reports, and for individual circumstances.

Before Beginning

Before beginning work on a term paper, you should know (1) the approximate length of the paper, (2) whether the instructor prefers a particular approach—does he want a review of the literature? or an evaluation of the ideas of others?—and (3) whether the instructor has any stylistic preferences. This information may or may not be stated explicitly by the instructor, but his preferences are often implicit in the way he makes the assignment.

Selecting the Topic

This is the first and usually the most important decision that must be made. There may be many good reasons for selecting a par-

ticular topic. You may want to explore a new idea; you may want to
investigate a topic that previously interested you; you may want
to investigate a topic that has vocational relevance for you; or
you may just be curious about something. Since a major term paper
requires a great deal of time and effort, a topic you find tedious
will increase the difficulty of the entire project. Be sure to select a topic that interests you.

   The length of a term paper also influences the selection of a
topic. Briefer papers require more specific and limited topics. In
addition, as you take increasingly advanced classes, the term-paper
topics tend to become increasingly specialized. The topic "Juvenile
delinquency" might be appropriate for a high school paper, but a
college paper would require a topic such as "The effects of impris-
onment and probation upon delinquents," "Family and personal background factors in delinquency," or "Job and educational opportunities for delinquents." Topics that are appropriate for graduate
students—such as "The experimental evidence of the effectiveness
of various forms of probation" or "A description of the retraining
center at State Reformatory for Boys"—may be too narrow for most
undergraduate papers.

   Of course, the slant of a paper may change after you begin to
do the reading. For example, you might begin with the topic "The
effects of automation on the worker," and then decide to limit it
to "The effects of automation on the factory worker." After doing
more reading, you might decide on a new focus—"The effects of
present-day automation on the factory worker, with implications for
the future." A paper on "Contemporary hospital care" may need to be
limited to "Contemporary psychiatric hospital care." "The scientific method in police detection in California" may need broadening
to "Scientific methods in police detection."

Scheduling the Work

   A very clever cartoon appeared in the 1950s showing two fig-
ures sprawled lazily in chairs, with the caption "Tomorrow we gotta
get organized." The cartoon became so popular that it eventually appeared on ashtrays, paper napkins, framed plaques, and so forth. Its
popularity undoubtedly reflected widespread feelings of inadequacy.
Perhaps at the time the cartoon was drawn, its creator was trying
to figure out the best way of organizing his work. And perhaps he
decided that it would be more fun to draw the cartoon. If so, the
cartoonist was doing what students everywhere do—they postpone the
necessary for the enjoyable.

   Term papers are assigned in addition to reading and other
activities, and they require special scheduling attention. One

approach is to establish a series of reasonable deadlines and stick
closely to them. Thus for a paper due in ten weeks you might wish
to set up a schedule something like this: Week 1, choose topic;
Week 5, complete most reading; Week 6, complete all additional
reading; Week 8, complete first thorough draft; Week 9, Day 2, complete final draft; Week 9, Day 4, complete final copy and go over
carefully for errors. Since things always seem to take longer than
it had originally seemed they should take, allowing more than
enough time for each stage is very useful.

Collecting Sources

Before jumping right into the reading and note taking, it's
a good idea to collect a number of references to give yourself
some idea of the range of books and articles relevant to your
topic. These can be obtained from lists of articles in such sources
as the *Readers' Guide to Periodical Literature*, the *New York Times
Index*, or a good encyclopedia. Sometimes you can find a book or an
article that contains a lengthy bibliography, occasionally with
helpful annotations. From these sources and from the library's card
catalog, you can compile an initial bibliography. Of course, since
the number of possible sources is likely to exceed by far the time
for reading, most students seek some basis for being selective.
(See Chapter 9 for more discussion of sources.)

Collecting Ideas

As you become more involved with your topics, you may come
across many good thoughts that seem worth including in your paper.
You may also receive suggestions from friends. Some authorities advise keeping a set of *idea cards*—index cards on which you can jot
down appealing ideas. Then, at a later time, you can dig these
cards out and integrate these ideas with your other materials.

Reading and Taking Notes

Once a bibliography has been started, the actual reading can
begin. At the same time, increased reading is likely to lead to
numerous bibliographic additions and some deletions. Reading for
term papers, just like all reading (see Chapter 7), need not be
done with the same thoroughness for each selection. Some articles
may require careful reading; others allow for skimming in parts;
and some materials can be skimmed in their entirety. It is useful

to begin your reading with a book or article that provides an overview of the topic and that introduces some of the more up-to-date
ideas, views, and research in the field.

Authorities agree on some aspects of note taking and disagree
on others. General agreement occurs on taking notes on lined index
cards, probably 5" × 8", and on placing the full bibliographic citation on each card to avoid having to return to the source later.
(Full citation for a book includes the name of the author, the
title of book, the date of publication, the location of the publisher, the name of the publisher, and the pages or chapters uti-
lized. For an article, the name of the publication and the volume
number need to be added, but you don't need the name or location of
the publisher. This information goes into your bibliography when
you have finished your paper.) Some experts encourage writing only
one idea on each card. Others suggest jotting down only summary
statements. Still others feel that it is best to write down as much
on each card as seems appropriate. Figure 10-1 shows two sample
note cards.

Books and articles, of course, are not the only sources of
information for term papers. Interviews, personal observations,
lecture materials, and informal conversations may all, under proper circumstances, provide acceptable sources. "Proper circumstances"
involve both the purpose of the report and the accuracy of the
writer in indicating the source of the information. For a research
paper, a program viewed on educational television is a perfectly
good source, provided the source is indicated in the paper. For a
less formal theme, the personal experiences of a close friend may
be totally appropriate to cite.

Outlining the Paper

For outlining the paper, I prefer the decimal method (see
Chapter 5), although most authorities adhere to the standard outline form. After carefully outlining the paper, go over all your
bibliography cards, idea cards, and interview cards, and assign
to each card one or more of the numbers on your decimal outline
form (or, of course, the letters and numbers from the standard outline form) to identify at what point or points in the paper they
are to be used. Then the cards can be placed in sequence so that
you can work through them as you write your paper. Those cards
bearing more than one note can be reinserted in the stack as many
times as necessary. An example of an outline is presented in
Figure 10-2.

Figure 10-1.   Reading notes for a term paper

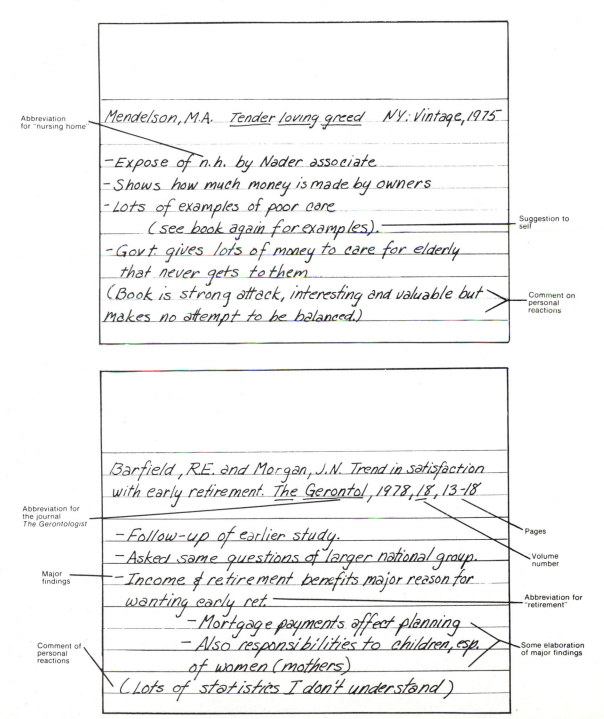

Abbreviation for "nursing home"

Mendelson, M.A.   *Tender loving greed*   NY: Vintage, 1975

−Expose of n.h. by Nader associate
− Shows how much money is made by owners
− Lots of examples of poor care
        (see book again for examples).
− Govt. gives lots of money to care for elderly
    that never gets to them
(Book is strong attack, interesting and valuable but
makes no attempt to be balanced.)

Suggestion to self

Comment on personal reactions

Abbreviation for the journal *The Gerontologist*

Barfield, R.E. and Morgan, J.N. *Trend in satisfaction*
with early retirement. The Gerontol, 1978, 18, 13-18

− Follow-up of earlier study.
− Asked same questions of larger national group.
− Income & retirement benefits major reason for
wanting early ret.
        − Mortgage payments affect planning
        − Also responsibilities to children, esp.
        of women (mothers)
(Lots of statistics I don't understand)

Pages

Volume number

Major findings

Abbreviation for "retirement"

Comment of personal reactions

Some elaboration of major findings

Writing the First Draft

If the outline is sufficiently detailed and if sufficient thinking and research have gone into the paper, the actual writing is not so difficult. Most instructors want an introductory statement to set the scene and a concluding statement to complete the paper. These features should be included in the outline.

Everyone has his or her own approach to writing the first draft. Some people write it quickly, without worrying about details or the final wording. Others work more slowly and painstakingly on the first draft. Some start with the introduction and work straight through to the concluding statements. Others work out particular sections and then piece the entire report together. One useful technique is to triple space the draft, if typing, or to skip every other line, if writing by hand, to allow ample room for extensive changes. Figure 10-2 shows some examples of material used in writing a term paper.

Figure 10-2. Materials for a term paper

WORKING WITH OLDER PERSONS AS A CAREER

Opening Sentence

Are you interested in an occupational field that is newly emerging, provides challenging work, is still dynamic and changing, and enables you to perform a service for people?

or

The demand for persons working with the elderly has increased dramatically in recent years and, it is generally anticipated, will increase in the future.

or

Work with a bunch of rigid, confused, senile old lumps? Not me. At least that was what I thought six months ago.

or

The contemporary attitude toward the demand for services for the elderly gives strong indication that opportunities will continue to improve, although rising costs do suggest the outside possibility of an economic backlash.

(Each of the sentences above provides a different approach to the topic—and you could certainly develop others. The first one appears directed toward an attempt at persuasion; the second seems to have an economic/personnel bias; the third is extremely personal; and the fourth provides a factual, journalistic beginning. The opening sentence in a term paper helps set the tone for the entire paper. It also should gain the attention of the reader and encourage him or her to read further.)

Outline

1. Introduction—give importance of work
   1.1 Brief historical background—difficult to obtain, check social work library
   1.2 Definitions—what does "old" mean; what is a gerontologist
2. Present demands—check federal, state, local programs and funding
   2.1 Opportunities—describe variety of kinds of jobs
       2.11 Recreation, social services, social administration, senior centers, etc.
   2.2 Variety of financial rewards, fringe benefits—take typical jobs
       2.21 Advancement potential
   2.3 Kinds of background and education appropriate
3. Type of personality desired—bring out inconsistencies
   3.1 Try to find research studies
   3.2 Or authorities (articles or else interview them)
   3.3 Own opinions
4. Factors to consider in accepting job
   4.1 Interest in program
   4.2 Potential to provide meaningful service
   4.3 Potential to build "small empire"
   4.4 Salary, benefits
   4.5 Type of older person and type of program
       4.51 Young old or old old
       4.52 Recreation, nutrition, senior center, counseling, etc.

5. Advantages of working with elderly—interview Ms. Harther, Rev. Pothier
   5.1 Challenge, new field, other aspects of personal satisfaction
   5.2 Jobs presently available, interest just beginning
   5.3 I enjoyed volunteering with older people, so find it exciting
6. Disadvantages
   6.1 Possible backlash, reduced funding
   6.2 Some work possibilities in nursing homes—I don't like
   6.3 People—must be certain to spend some time with my own age
   6.4 Many jobs based on government funding, may not be permanent
7. Summarize pros and cons, integrate with own ideas
8. Conclusion
9. Summary statement

(Notice the informality of the outline, which includes both the usual outline material plus several reminders to the writer. This outline is for your own benefit and can be as complete as you wish. Also, it can use any style or form you wish, and you don't have to look up spelling or grammar at this point.)

References

Butler, R. N. Public interest report number 11. New colleges for all ages. *Aging and Human Development*, 1974, *5*, 107–110.

Kalish, R. A. Manpower requirements in social gerontology. *The Gerontologist*, 1968, *2*, 215–220.

Riegel, K. F. History of psychological gerontology. In J. E. Birren & K. W. Schaie (Eds.), *Handbook of the psychology of aging*. New York: Van Nostrand Reinhold, 1977. Pp. 70–102.

Schulz, J. H. *The economics of aging*. Belmont, Calif.: Wadsworth, 1976.

Storandt, M., Siegler, I. C., & Elias, M. F. (Eds.). *The clinical psychology of aging*. New York: Plenum, 1978.

U.S. Department of Health, Education, and Welfare. *Working with older people: A guide to practice. Vol. I: The practitioner and the elderly*. Washington, D.C.: Government Printing Office, 1966 and other dates.

(This partial bibliography shows the different types
of source material available in the campus library. Three
of the references are books put out by publishing compa-
nies, one book is published by the government, and two are
journal articles.)

Revising the Paper

After completing the first draft, you may wish to read it over
for sense and meaning, writing in minor corrections and jotting
down notes for making major changes later. Most students probably
want nothing to do with the paper for at least a couple of days.
Whatever your immediate response, you are well advised to leave the
paper alone for two or three days before returning for revising,
writing the final draft, and polishing. This permits you to approach the paper from a fresh point of view. Revision may be a matter of making changes on the original draft, writing a new draft,
or combining the two by a scissors-and-staple job. At least one
more thorough draft is usually necessary before preparing the
final form.

Either before the final draft or just following it, you might
ask a friend to read the paper, in order to pick up errors in
grammar and spelling, to suggest sections where the reading is not
smooth, and to point out unclear ideas and important omissions. If
this is not possible reading the paper aloud to yourself is a reasonable alternative.

Preparing the Final Copy

Basically, few changes are made in moving from the final draft
to the final copy, although changes in wording and mechanics are
still very appropriate. Typed papers seem to receive better grades
than handwritten ones. Even though this is certainly unfair, it
probably reflects the better impression made by the typed paper and
the extra effort required to read the handwriting many students display. However, a *neatly* handwritten paper usually fares well. Making
a carbon copy or xeroxing your paper is both a wise precaution and
a guarantee that you will have a good copy of the paper for your
own future reference.

Part of the preparation of the final copy is checking your
footnotes and bibliographic citations. Footnotes are used to indicate either sources or explanatory material not appropriate for
inclusion in the body of the paper. Bibliographic sources may be

cited in footnotes or listed at the end of the paper, indicated by numbers or by the author's name and the date of publication.

Proofreading

Because so many term papers are completed in the small hours of the morning, students may lack the energy and the will to do any proofreading at all. However, a final careful reading, perhaps after a few hours of sleep, may catch minor errors, omitted sentences or paragraphs, misstated ideas, or confusing passages.

WHAT A TERM PAPER IS NOT

A term paper is not a collection of quotations from the works of other people. At worst, this is plagiarism, or stealing other peoples' work. Plagiarism occurs when writers credit themselves for what someone else wrote or said. Giving credit to the proper source is considered one of the responsibilities of a competent author. Some students fill their papers with quotations but avoid the charge of plagiarism by using quotation marks and indicating their sources. In these cases they are not plagiarizing—merely doing a very poor job.

Nor is a term paper a polemic. That is, except in rare instances, the term paper is not supposed to present biased and distorted evidence—or even prejudicially selected evidence—or to espouse one point of. view in a propagandistic fashion.

In essence, then, a term paper requires research, creativity, organization, writing skills, and knowledge of writing mechanics. Success in college and in your career after college is, of course, possible without having competence in these abilities, but there is no doubt that the capacity to produce a good term paper is one of the skills you will learn in college.

SUMMARY OF IMPORTANT IDEAS

1. Writing differs from speaking in that writing cannot use tone of voice, pauses, gestures, or facial expressions to help communicate. Writing uses more traditional word forms and grammatical structure, and writing is more self-conscious and more artificial.

2. Term papers provide the opportunity to pursue a particular, topic in depth, to learn about a variety of source materials, to work independently, and to consider new ideas.

3. Different professors expect different types of term papers. Some wish high levels of scholarship, while others are more concerned with creativity or breadth of knowledge.

4. A well-written term paper has something to say, supports its points with good research and intelligent thought, and uses a literate style and proper mechanics.

5. Proper selection of a term-paper topic is the first major decision.

6. Term papers require more scheduling consideration than most other college tasks.

7. Subsequent steps in doing a term paper include obtaining sources, collecting ideas, reading and taking notes, and—eventually—outlining and writing the paper. The importance of the outlining step is often underestimated by students.

8. Term papers require not only an original draft but also revisions and, eventually, a good final copy that has been thoroughly proofread.

EXERCISE

Getting the Background for a Term Paper

The following assignment can be done with an actual term paper in mind or on any topic agreeable to you and your instructor.

1. Select a topic:

_____

Why did you select this particular topic?   _____

_____

2. Where can you go for material? (List both people and places.)

a. _____

b. _____

c. _____

d. _____

3. List four periodicals you might find useful as sources:

a. _____

b. _____

c. _____

d. _____

4. In using the library card catalog, what topics would you investigate?

a. _____

b. _____

c. _____

d. _____

e. _____

f. _____

Continued

5. Would your style be formal or informal? Amusing or serious? Why?

_____

_____

_____

_____

_____

_____

6. Jot down a couple of ideas you might incorporate into your paper.

_____

_____

_____

_____

_____

_____

_____

7. List ten books and articles which you might use as references. Include author, title, name of magazine or name of publisher, date, pages used for reference (if necessary). Be certain that your list includes at least two articles from professional journals, two articles from popular magazines, and two books.

_____

_____

_____

_____

_____

_____

_____

_____

_____

_____

_____

_____

_____

_____

OBJECTIVES

1. To suggest procedures to help you study specific fields: mathematics, literature and the fine arts, and the sciences.

Chapter 11

Studying Special Subjects

APPROACHING MATHEMATICS*

"I just can't do math."
"I hate numbers."
"People have too many numbers attached to them. It's dehumanizing."

For many reasons, a substantial proportion of students have difficulty with numbers. Some women have trouble with math because as young girls they were taught that "boys are good in math and girls are not." They develop the notion that to be good in math is to be unfeminine, just as some men feel that to enjoy art or classical music is unmasculine. But many men also have difficulty in higher math. Indeed, when the faculty members of a particular department decide there are too many students majoring in their program, they merely need to increase the math requirements and their majors quickly fall away.

One cause of problems with math is failing to keep up-to-date in your math courses. Since math builds on itself, missing a few classes or a few assignments makes the subsequent classes or assignments extremely difficult. Once they have fallen behind, students are intimidated by their own confusion and see the task of catching up as overwhelming.

*I would like to acknowledge the contributions to this section provided by the late Frances E. Davis, Department of Mathematics, Leeward Community College, Hawaii, and Diane Resek, Department of Mathematics, San Francisco State University.

Scholars and educators have combined their efforts to understand why students fear and avoid numbers and, more importantly, to develop ways to enable them to overcome their fears. These experts have concluded that it is the fear that makes math difficult rather than anything intrinsic in the math itself. You might examine your attitudes toward math and toward numbers, in order to understand better your ability to do the work.

In mathematics, one thing that tends to confuse and intimidate students is the use of symbols and formulas. Although they look strange and mysterious, they are merely a method of shorthand invented by mathematicians, scientists, and engineers to make it possible to express complicated ideas in a simple form. Once you are familiar with the symbols, the mystery disappears.

The most essential process in mathematics is analysis. When you have a problem to solve or want to know why certain things happen under certain conditions, you need to analyze the relevant information. Analysis tells you which tools to use and how to use them. Thus, the more math you learn, the more tools you have and the greater is your ability to use them.

Studying Mathematics

To be able to learn mathematics successfully, you must have a solid background of facts. If you have trouble performing high-school-level arithmetic processes, get a remedial math book and spend a specified period each day in review. This review is especially important for those of you who have not had a math course in several years. Not only have you probably forgotten a great deal, but today's books and instructors approach math in different ways.

To get maximum gain from a self-study of remedial math, work the simpler problems until they become second nature. If particular phases of the elementary work are difficult for you, work hardest on them and, if necessary, get extra help from either an instructor or a math tutoring center.

A few students find mathematical concepts easy to learn. Most students, however, have to spend considerable time on math, and the concepts do not fall into place until they have been used over and over again. Learning mathematics requires regular and efficient use of study time. You will usually find it necessary to spend at least two hours outside of class for every hour in class.

In studying math, one superficial reading is not enough. You may have to read over the section five or six times, and you are likely to find that it takes as long to read and comprehend three pages of math as 30 pages of some other texts. When you read, have lots of scratch paper available, and work out the examples as you go. You might also wish to develop a notebook or card file of terms, concepts, and formulas that are particularly important.

In addition to working the examples, look over your class notes and rework the problems presented by the instructor to be certain you have all the procedures firmly in mind. At this point, you should be able to work out the book problems on your own. If you find that you frequently need to look back to the book, then you don't understand the process adequately.

Then start on the assigned problems. Again, if you have to make constant reference to the book or to your notes, you don't fully understand the concepts, and you're likely to have difficulty later. Unless you thoroughly comprehend the theories that you're applying, your ability to solve problems is soon lost. Depending entirely on class lectures and demonstrations is not enough either. Watching someone else perform doesn't replace actually performing yourself. A balance of textbook study, review of notes, strict attention during class, and actual practice in working problems is necessary. Of these, the most easily ignored and probably the most important is working the problems.

An excellent time to study is shortly after the class session. At that time, it is easier to assimilate the new facts and to understand the text. If some point defies understanding, there is still time to visit the math tutoring center (check to see if your college has one and when you can go there) or the instructor for help. When assigned work is put off until the night before the next class, it's too easy just to work through the problems, without spending the essential time in review and study.

One of the most difficult things for many students is the solution of word problems. The more math you take, the more likely you are to be confronted with verbal problems rather than simple numerical problems. Once again, the more problems you actually do, the clearer the concepts will become and the easier it will be to do subsequent problems. However, if you do have difficulty, don't hesitate to get tutoring help before your frustration becomes too great. Make certain that you are capable of doing the problems on your own before you decide you've finished the assignment.

Studying For and Taking Examinations

How to study for math examinations is another major concern, since the procedures aren't the same as those for other courses. The following are a few suggestions:

1. Read over the text material, and go over any class notes. Make a list of all important definitions, formulas, and theorems

that you should memorize. Then memorize them! If you've been studying properly and using the formulas and theorems, this task should
not be difficult, and it's essential.

   2. Look over the illustrative problems in the text and in
your notes. Work at least one of each type without referring to the
examples. Then check your work for accuracy.

   3. Review any problems that were assigned as homework and
were checked by the instructor. This step will give you an idea of
how the instructor expects things to be done and of how he or she
rates each topic. Naturally, the more problems assigned and class
time spent on any topic, the more likely it is that questions on
that material will be included on the examination.

   4. When studying for the final exam, go over all previous
tests very carefully. Rework any problems you didn't understand or
didn't solve properly.

   During the examination, you should (1) look over the entire
list of questions, (2) budget your time, (3) make certain that all
solutions are properly labeled, and (4) spend the last few minutes
checking your work, making certain that no problem or part of a
problem has been omitted and that the simple arithmetic is correct.

   Mathematics is one of the most important fields of study. It
shares many of the characteristics found in any other area of
study, but some approaches to math are more unique. For some people,
overcoming their fear of math or their antagonism toward numbers is
the first step to successful study.

     THE STUDY AND ENJOYMENT OF LITERATURE
     AND THE FINE ARTS

   Literature and the fine arts can be enjoyed both through participating in the creative process personally or through reading,
listening to, or watching the creativity and performance of others.
For any given art form, some people prefer to participate, while
others would rather be spectators.

   We aren't really certain of the best way to help people become
effective and observant critics and appreciative spectators. Here
we can draw an analogy between art forms and athletes. We can
teach people to play Rhapsody in Blue or to sink a lay-up shot, but
we cannot teach them to enjoy piano music or have fun at a basketball game. There is, of course, reason to believe that learning
something about the arts will increase a person's appreciation of
them. Can you imagine how difficult it would be for someone totally
unfamiliar with baseball to appreciate the finesse needed to pick a
runner off third base? How many Americans can fully appreciate the
skill of a matador? If learning about baseball or bullfighting

increases one's enjoyment and critical ability as a spectator, it stands to reason that learning about ceramics or modern dance would have the same outcome.

Often a student, after encountering a modern painting or sculpture, a strange-sounding poem, or an experimental film, is heard to moan "For crying out loud, what is that?" One noted English instructor has an apt suggestion: "When you don't understand it, sit back and let it happen." In other words, do not look for subtle meanings or hidden messages. Just try to live with it for a while and get the feel of it. We tend to reject new approaches, whether in politics, religion, or art. Modern art styles are not always pleasing or pretty, but they're often not meant to be. Art is a form of communication, and some writers, composers, or painters do not wish to communicate a sense of prettiness; they may wish to frighten, to horrify, to irritate, to amuse, or to arouse to action.

Although the emphasis in college is often on spectator roles, actual participation in creative arts can be even more satisfying. Here again information is helpful, but experience and sensitivity are also necessary. You can learn the techniques of figure drawing or television-script writing, but you will also need to spend a lot of time with it. The successful professional artist has developed effective self-discipline. Amateurs can decide to write only when the mood strikes, but professionals don't need to wait—the mood is either there much of the time or else they find ways to create the mood.

Of course, few people become professional artists or writers or actors, but many pursue these activities through amateur participation or as spectators. However, people can enjoy art forms at any level of expertise and with any degree of participation.

The Study Process

Studying art courses such as art history or music appreciation is much like studying any other course. Studying for creative-art courses, on the other hand, involves a combination of practice, observation, discussion, criticism by others, reading, and so forth. Some of the skills discussed in this book are quite relevant to the creative-art classes in college, while others are much less so.

The study of literature is of particular importance, however, for two reasons: First, a large proportion of college students take at least one course in literature, and, second, the profit and enjoyment of reading is widely recognized. The SQ3R method can be applied to all forms of nontextbook literature, except for poetry, with very little difficulty.

Survey. Read any material about the selection, including historical background, the author's biography, critics' interpretations, and so forth. However, do *not* skim the piece itself.

Question. Write down from one to several questions, selecting those you feel are particularly important.

Read. This step is the same in any type of studying.

Recall. Recall and recite the answers to your questions. You will be answering several questions now, instead of just one as with the textbook SQ3R. Jot the answers down.

Review. Review your SQ3R notes.

Reading the questions on page 173 probably suggests that more than a single reading is necessary to provide intelligent answers to the questions. Re-reading reveals ideas that might have been missed earlier and increases the depth and breadth of understanding.

Reading for Relaxation

A note must be added on reading for pleasure and relaxation. Some students make the mistake of associating all good literature with the academic process. Then, when they wish to "get away from it all," they feel they must read immature, unchallenging books. Hundreds of good, readable books are available, many in inexpensive paperbound form, that provide enjoyable reading. These books range from *Crime and Punishment* to *Bridge over the River Kwai*, from short story collections of Anatole France, Edgar Allan Poe, and Ernest Hemingway to the better science fiction stories, from *Hamlet* to Arthur Miller, from Keats to Rod McKuen, and include literature that is widely accepted as high quality as well as selections that are less competently written.

If you have any doubt about the type of reading that would be appropriate to your desires and also worth your while, a librarian, English teacher, or reading specialist will always be glad to make suggestions.

Applying the Question Step of SQ3R to Literature

Questions to ask of fiction and drama:

1. What is the theme of the book or play?
2. What is the most important plot? What are the subplots? Do they all seem to fit into the theme naturally?
3. Briefly sketch the leading characters. Is the motivation for their actions realistic?
4. What do setting and atmosphere contribute?
5. Describe the style. Does the author maintain the same style throughout the selection?
6. What sort of symbolism is used?
7. Would you recommend this book to someone else? Why?

Questions to ask of nonfiction:

1. Who is the author and what is his or her background? (A geologist writing about geology can usually be considered an authority. The same geologist writing about personal political convictions becomes a layman who may know no more about the subject than you do.)
2. When was the book written? (A book on World War I written in 1919 and one on the same war written in 1970 would probably use the same facts but would interpret them in a different fashion.)
3. What is the general viewpoint expressed by the author?
4. What are the chief ideas in each chapter? (It is a good idea to summarize each chapter as you finish it, rather than wait until completing the book. In your notebook jot down these points. Three or four ideas will briefly cover the chapter.)
5. Would you recommend this book to another reader? Why? (Consider the style of writing, special illustrative material, use of examples to clarify difficult points, and the manner in which the author has communicated with the reader—directly or indirectly, formally or informally, and so on.)

Studying Poetry

1. Read the poem over. What mood do you sense?
2. Reread the poem—this time aloud. Listen for the rhythm
    of the lines and enjoy the sequence of sound.
3. Study the images that the poet uses to achieve various
    levels of meaning. In *Fog*, by Carl Sandburg, you have
    the image of fog. To express how the fog moves, Sand-
    burg compares it to a cat. Fog is silent; it moves on
    little cat feet; it finally moves on.
4. Look at the words. Remember, many words have more than
    one meaning. Be sure you know which meaning the poet
    intended.
5. Look for symbols that must be understood. The subject
    of symbols is very difficult to discuss briefly. But
    more mature poets try to give multiple meanings to
    their words and ideas. A cat, for instance, may be
    more than a soft, furry creature. It may symbolize a
    woman with catlike qualities, a small tiger represent-
    ing in miniature the actions of the jungle creature,
    or, as in many tales of mystery and terror, it may
    represent the hidden, silent evil of the night. The
    meanings you perceive will depend on how much you see
    within the poem.

    Names of mythical gods and goddesses or names of
famous people usually have some extension of meaning also.
When the name of Jove, Ceres, or Tantalus appears, for instance, you can be sure that the writer wishes you to remember what aspect of nature, what particular powers, or,
perhaps, what mythological life events are associated with
these gods and goddesses. If you look up this information,
you will find that in one word you have been given a great
deal of meaning.

MAKING SENSE OF SCIENCE*

Science has become one of the major forces of modern society.
The scientific approach is used, or is claimed to be in use, by
business, politics, agriculture, technology, architecture—even
housekeeping.

    The prestige attached to the scientific approach is due to the
extraordinary successes resulting from the work of scientists. We

*Based on material by the late Albert J. Bernatowicz.

have increased our factual information about the world and our theo-
retical understanding of it to a degree that permits considerable
control and manipulation. Yet the ability to control or change
nature does not mean that we are competent to use that ability
properly.

Three main values of studying the sciences may be stated.
First, and most important in the long run, you can develop a thorough awareness of the scientific approach. What are the techniques,
attitudes, and methods that have been successful in science? How
can they be applied to areas not traditionally considered as sciences? How can you think as a scientist—even though you may never
use a laboratory?

Second, you need competence in the sciences to judge the de-
sirability of employing the discoveries of science. Science makes
possible the partial control of nature; applying this control is
usually the job of technologies such as medicine, engineering, or
industry. Leaders at the national or even community level face the
problem of how to control nature through science. Examples of such
political decisions are those relating to forest conservation,
nuclear testing, air-pollution control, and genetic research.

More immediate questions of control require decisions from
everyone; for example, whether to get flu shots, to give up smoking,
or to buy bread with added vitamins are all policy decisions that
individuals must make for themselves. Competence in making these
decisions depends on a critical understanding of the claims attrib-
uted to science: How confident are scientists of their findings? Do
they actually furnish adequate proof? What are the limitations of
their findings? Do scientists make claims beyond the boundaries of
their scientific knowledge?

Third, of course, you must know some of the content of science
before applying it. Here the average person completely confuses
science with technology. The content of science courses rarely includes "how to fix a carburetor" or "how to reduce safely without
giving up food." These are some of the infinite number of specific
applications and selecting any particular ones to teach would be
pointless. Also, in many cases, specific applications of science
become outdated so rapidly that teaching them in a college science
course is useless.

The real importance of the third value of studying sciences
lies in learning basic facts, principles, and theories that enable
you to understand some of the writing of specialists, to reject
pseudoscientific advertisements, and to recognize ideas that may
be practical in home or business. An elementary school teacher, for
example, must know enough about the sciences to answer questions
intelligently. He or she must be able to set up simple demonstrations in the physical and life sciences, to understand the meaning

and limitations of intelligence testing, and to recognize the effects that exercise may have on the health of a child. The person
in business needs to know about market research, quality control,
machine tolerances, and chemical composition of products, and
computer technology. Of course, if you are anticipating working
in any of the sciences or fields closely related to them, you must
know the method and content of your own field thoroughly and have
some background in the other sciences.

Sciences and the Scientific Method

Although it is impossible to classify the sciences with any
degree of precision, three major categories provide a fairly satisfactory breakdown. Each of these areas makes use of the scientific
method plus a great deal of creative thinking and considerable
knowledge of principles and details.

Physical Sciences. Studies of nonorganic materials, such
as those conducted in physics, chemistry, and geology,
may be classed as the physical sciences.

Life Sciences. Botany, zoology, bacteriology, and some
areas of psychology study the living organism and are
therefore called life sciences.

Behavioral and Social Sciences. Sociology, economics,
anthropology, political science, some aspects of history
and geography, and other areas of psychology study individual behavior and the effects of human relationships.
These may be termed behavioral and social sciences.

The various sciences differ in the detailed use of the scientific method, but all include use of six essential steps:

1. Recognizing, with some precision, what the problem is.
2. Obtaining background—assimilating what has been done
   previously.
3. Setting up a hypothesis (a prediction of the logical
   consequences) or set of hypotheses based on the previous step.
4. Determining the procedure to follow in testing the
   hypothesis.
5. Gathering the data by the chosen procedure to test
   the hypothesis.

6. Analyzing the data to see how they bear upon the
    hypothesis to discover any additional implications.

Sometimes a seventh step—that of verifying the study by re-
peating it—is included.

Your Approach to the Sciences

You may have noticed the importance of creative ability in the
scientific methods. Steps 1, 3, and 4 are based almost entirely on
creativity; all of the steps are dependent to some degree upon cre-
ativie thinking. Technicians are needed and are valuable; however,
creative ability distinguishes the true scientist from a good
technician.

Many students complain that the sciences demand too much memorizing. Often these are the students who fail to see the larger
principles that tie details together in a meaningful fashion. For
example, you may learn three pieces of information: (1) people who
dislike their employers are poor workers; (2) people who dislike
their teachers are poor students; (3) people who dislike their
parents are likely to be unhappy. You can easily see the underlying
idea that people who resent authority are likely to be poor in the
activities related to that particular authority. Now you can draw
some of your own implications; for example, football players who
dislike their coach are likely to be less effective players.

A general principle at one level may become a detail needed in
the development of a still more general principle. In the physical
sciences, Newton's Three Laws are considered fairly broad principles:

>   Law I.   Objects in uniform motion or at rest remain so
>   unless acted upon by a force.
>   Law II. The acceleration or change in motion of an ob-
>   ject is directly proportional to the force
>   acting upon the object and inversely propor-
>   tional to the mass of the object.
>   Law III. For every action, there is an equal and oppo-
>   site reaction.

Before Newton, Galileo recognized that these principles applied to objects on earth, including falling objects. But Newton
found that the same principles applied when he considered the earth
and the moon as falling toward each other. From this principle, not
only was the Law of Universal Gravitation recognized, but an even
greater principle—that the laws of motion apply not only to earth
but also to the whole universe—was discovered. Few students recog-

nize the immense scope of this generalization. For 2000 years before Newton, it had been thought that different principles applied
to celestial bodies. As a direct consequence of his discovery, we
now have space satellites and the probability of interplanetary
travel.

You need to know the details in order to understand the principles. It is more important to understand the principles, however,
because a person who understands them finds that many of the details become obvious. As new information becomes available, the
principles may be altered to include the new material. If you understand the principles, you will be able to understand the changes.
For those who know only the details, new information will be confusing.

The principles for studying the sciences are the same as those
for studying other areas. SQ3R can still apply to most reading.
SQ3R will be a considerable asset in learning principles as opposed
to facts. Underlining and other symbols as described in Chapter 6
can also be used. Notetaking (Chapter 5), time scheduling (Chapter
3), and study conditions (Chapter 4) are the same in studying the
sciences. One possible change is that you may wish to spend more
than 90 minutes at one time in studying science courses, especially
those in which laboratory assignments are involved.

In some cases memorizing will be essential. As in all fields,
certain details must be learned thoroughly. These might include a
formula in physics, a definition in psychology, or a genus name in
zoology. You need to be familiar with the vocabulary of the science,
although this may take extra effort. You will undoubtedly come
across many new words (enzymes, sociometrics, valence) and many old
words with new meanings (personality, work, respiration). These
must be learned not by rote but in terms of their meanings and applications. The index, the glossary, or a dictionary may be needed
to clarify meanings. Each field of study has its own dictionary
that will give you technical definitions that may not appear in a
standard dictionary.

Laboratories

Most of the physical sciences, many of the life sciences, and
some of the behavioral and social sciences include laboratory work
as part of the class requirements. Laboratory experiments or demonstrations enable you to become familiar with the methods of the
science, with the difficulties in doing research, and with some of
the content. Since content is not the sole objective, you should
not be disturbed if you do not learn as much content from three
hours of laboratory work as from three hours of lecture. Reporting

laboratory work is similar to writing a brief term paper, except that the outline is usually given at the beginning. Some of the common errors students make with laboratory assignments include (1) messiness—too much erasure creates a bad impression on the grader; (2) inaccuracies—everyone occasionally misspells words and calculates numbers incorrectly, but the good student will correct them by proofreading; (3) poor diagrams—you don't need to be an artist in order to be neat; and (4) rigid thinking—a good student will go beyond the immediate data to discuss implications, possibility and magnitude of errors, and ways of improving the study.

In Conclusion

Studying the sciences is essentially like studying any other course. The use of SQ3R, proper note taking, time scheduling, and study conditions apply equally to science courses. Memorizing certain information, understanding principles and details, and doing laboratory assignments carefully have their counterparts in other courses also.

SUMMARY OF IMPORTANT IDEAS

1. For many reasons, a substantial proportion of students have trouble with mathematics.
2. The most essential process in math is analysis.
3. Understanding math requires a knowledge of both facts and concepts.
4. Actually doing the mathematical problems is the best way to study math.
5. Enjoyment of literature and the fine arts can occur both as a participant and as a spectator.
6. Studying literature can be helped by applying a variation of SQ3R.
7. The sciences all use the scientific method but apply it in different ways.
8. Like math, science requires knowledge of both facts and concepts.
9. Laboratory work is important in most of the sciences.

REFERENCES

Anderson, R. C. Educational psychology. *Annual Review of Psychology*, 1967, *18*, 129–164.

Blair, G. M. *Diagnostic and remedial teaching*. New York: Macmillan, 1956.

Carter, J. F., & Van Matre, N. H. Note taking versus note having. *Journal of Educational Psychology*, 1975, *67*, 900–904.

DelGiorno, W., Jenkins, J. R., & Bausell, R. B. Effects of recitation on the acquisition of prose. *Journal of Educational Research*, 1974, *67*, 293–294.

Ellis, H. *The transfer of learning*. New York: Macmillan, 1965.

Fisher, J. L., & Harris, M. B. Effect of note taking and review on recall. *Journal of Educational Psychology*, 1973, *65*, 321–325.

Fox, L. Effecting the use of efficient study habits. *Journal of Mathetics*, 1962, *1*, 75–86.

Fraser, L. T., & Schwartz, B. J. Effect of question production and answering on prose recall. *Journal of Educational Psychology*, 1975, *67*, 628–635.

Gordon, I. J. *How to be a good discusser*. Program Guide Series. B'nai B'rith Youth Organization, pamphlet, undated.

Harris, A. J. *How to increase reading ability* (3rd ed.). New York: Longmans Green, 1956.

Holmes, A. J. Factors underlying major reading disabilities at the college level. *Genetic Psychology Monographs*, 1954, *49*, 3–95.

Hovland, C. I. Human learning and retention. In S. S. Stevens (Ed.), *Handbook of experimental psychology*. New York: Wiley, 1951.

Kalish, R. A. *Late adulthood: Perspectives on human development*. Monterey, Calif.: Brooks/Cole, 1975.

Kastenbaum, R. L. On the meaning of time in later life. *Journal of Genetic Psychology*, 1966, *109*, 9–25.

Robinson, F. P. *Effective study* (Rev. ed.). New York: Harper & Row, 1961.

Smith, S. S. *The command of words* (Rev. ed.). New York: Crowell, 1949.

Strang, R., McCullough, C. M., & Traxler, A. E. *Improvement of reading* (4th ed.). New York: McGraw-Hill, 1967.

Tinker, M. A. Effect of angular alignment upon readability of print. *Journal of Educational Psychology*, 1956, *47*, 358–363.

Wittrock, M. C., & Lumsdaine, A. A. Instructional psychology. *Annual Review of Psychology*, 1977, *28*, 417–459.

INDEX